RESPONSIBILITY REBELLION

RESPONSIBILITY REBELLION

AN UNCONVENTIONAL APPROACH
TO PERSONAL EMPOWERMENT

KAIN RAMSAY
WITH CINZIA DUBOIS

HOUNDSTOOTH
PRESS

RESPONSIBILITY REBELLION
An Unconventional Approach to Personal Empowerment

ISBN   978-1-5445-0912-9   *Hardcover*
        978-1-5445-0913-6   *Paperback*
        978-1-5445-0911-2   *Ebook*
        978-1-5445-1443-7   *Audiobook*

CONTENTS

INTRODUCTION

THERE ARE VERY FEW PEOPLE IN THIS WORLD WHO haven't, at one point in their life, had an extremely messed up relationship with themselves. All relationships are complicated and require effort to maintain; but unlike familial, platonic, and romantic relationships, the relationship we have with ourselves doesn't bend in the same way. Like it or not, you're stuck with yourself. Any other relationship is negotiable, whether familial, platonic, or romantic—in any of those scenarios, you *can* walk away if you need to. Your relationship with yourself, on the other hand, is permanent. You can hardly walk away from yourself or talk things out another day if things become unpleasant, and that's where the problem lies.

We've all heard of those quirky phrases which warn you that 'if you don't love yourself, nobody else can either' which, if you're anything like me, you've gagged at in the past. Why? Because you have evidence to the contrary. You've been in *plenty* of romantic relationships during periods of your life when you hated or disliked yourself (heck, you probably got married during that period of your life); your parents love you; your siblings and cousins love you; you have friends who tell you they love you all the time; and your cat loves you more than anything else in the world! Unfortunately, the irritatingly fluffy catchphrases about self-love and acceptance we see in garishly curly, glittery fonts on the front of sparkly tumbler cups have an essence of truth to them, albeit in a less romanticised and more grounded and psychology-textbook kind of way.

I've met a lot of people who dislike or even hate who they are or how they are, or what they've done in life (or haven't done). I've met hundreds who resent when and where they were born and who they were born to, the opportunities life never afforded them, or the looks and skills they were never genetically 'gifted' with. *Why can't I be like X?* they ask themselves, or *Why can't I have their life? Why don't I look like them? Why aren't I as successful as that?*

Rather than seeing other people as symbols or evidence for their own potential in life, some people fall into a comparison trap and see themselves as fundamentally flawed and incapable of being anything other than who they are today. They're victims of the body they were given, the nationality and class they were born into, and their intellectual capabilities and personality. Other people go to an extreme to make themselves anew by working solely on external factors: they dye their hair, grow a beard, spend thousands on new clothes and things for their house, buy a new car, over-exercise at the gym, spend thousands on plastic surgery, change careers, go back to university, move to different countries, lose a lot of weight, adopt a new religion, join a new society, have another child, or get a divorce and start dating someone new.

None of these things are bad. Self-improvement can take all

forms, and most of us are lucky enough to live in a society in which we have the liberty to become rich enough to afford these additions in life. Having plastic surgery because you want to doesn't make you any less of a person, and the same goes for losing weight, gaining weight, buying a new car, changing careers, or leaving a relationship which isn't making you happy. That's all great; there's nothing wrong with any of that. The problem is when we see these things in society and determine them to be an answer to our internal issues.

Despite what posters, movies, television shows, and commercials tell us, 'treating yourself' to material goods isn't an act of self-care and love. Self-love isn't a monetary transaction and self-care shouldn't involve price tags, but we're playing a part in a system which wants us to believe otherwise so we'll keep investing in it, in the hope that it'll make us a more fulfilled, happier, and better person.

When we fail to see ourselves as a personified relationship, all we see when we look in the mirror is a lonely lump of clay which needs defining and adding to in order to mean something. We become duped into naively buying into this heinous idea that money, fame, status, and things will make us better people. If we invest into looking better we'll be more significant, we'll feel better, we'll be better, and ultimately, more people will like and admire us. What you need to learn sooner rather than later is that no one in this world can out-love the self-hatred you have. The only way you can escape your toxic relationship with yourself is to work on rebuilding it into a stronger, healthier one. My mission in this book is to open your mind and make you realise that the way you see things in life, yourself included, isn't actually how things are. The only way you can achieve this is by learning how to master yourself and rebel against the messages which tell you that you aren't enough. Mastering yourself means being able to see things more clearly and accepting that your concept of 'reality' is nothing more than your perceptions of it.

People either want to control their own lives or they want to control how other people see them. People who master themselves live an empowered life. They don't need to rely on external validation because their self-esteem and self-worth aren't tentatively balanced on the fleeting opinions of others. Those with personal mastery don't miss out on opportunities and relationships in life, and they aren't suffocated and chained to the detrimental core beliefs they adopted about themselves in childhood. Personal mastery comes out of accepting that things are *not* the way we think they are and investing in the belief that everything can be changed or achieved.

If we never build a relationship with ourselves, we end up buying our own affections in the hope that it will either (a) make us like ourselves more, or (b) make other people like us so much that their validation drowns out our self-hatred and we forget about it. Both of these outcomes are impossible; no amount of wealth will ever make you like yourself. You may have had a relationship where one person tries to buy another person's affection. It's a notorious trait of a people pleaser, but none of us is immune to the behaviour. Perhaps you bought a packet of biscuits for that colleague in your office who always gives you the cold shoulder to try to thaw their icy indifference or bought an expensive piece of jewellery for a partner you fought with. Or, if you've been on the receiving end, perhaps you had a parent who overcompensated for your broken or nonexistent relationship by buying you tons of toys for your birthday or Christmas. Or maybe someone at school who you didn't really like constantly gave you their sweets until you felt obliged to play with them. You know as well as anyone that buying your way into a relationship is the most hollow and insincere approach you can take, but that's how most people build their relationship with themselves.

Most of us only like ourselves when we give in and 'treat ourselves' to new things; we constantly try to appease our self-loathing inner monologue with clothes, food, gadgets, television, makeup, surgery, fancy cars, watches, heck, even stationery. Yet when we buy ourselves these things, we're no better than that annoying kid in class who you really don't like coming up to you and beginning to hang out with you in exchange for some fizzy cola bottles or a bar of chocolate. You loathe the idea of accepting them into your life on such a shallow basis, yet you do it anyway because you like fizzy sweets, new clothes, fast cars, and cool gadgets. So, you put up with yourself in exchange for nice things, until the novelty wears off and you have to go back out to the shops looking for something nice to give yourself in exchange for temporary inner peace and self-acceptance once again.

Most people find the concept of talking to themselves as though they were a child/their best friend difficult because of the cognitive dissonance they have between their external relationships and their internal relationship. Our minds work really hard to convince us we're different from other people, so much that the most common psychology advice doesn't apply to us. The special snowflake syndrome is not just a mil-lennial problem; we treat ourselves differently to how we treat others because we think of ourselves as unique beings whose struggles are harder, whose circumstances are unparalleled, and whose wrongdoings, failures, flaws, and faults are more severe than any universal human fallibilities. Your unique degree of hopelessness is why you call yourself all the things you wouldn't even call your worst enemy: *I'm a pathetic loser*; *I'm fat, ugly and worthless*; *I'm a scrawny, weak waste of space*; *I'm too stupid to do anything with my life*; *I'm a failure and always will be*; *I'll never accomplish anything in life*.

People have a lot of nasty stuff to say about themselves because negative bias is construed in our minds as being a positive motivational tool which, yes, in core psychology, it is. Negative bias kept humans alive in terms of evolutionary theory, but negative bias doesn't translate well when it's used perpetually. Whilst being unhappy with your figure may initiate negative self-talk which prompts you to join a gym and eat healthier, perpetually belittling and condescending your appearance and body shape isn't going to empower you to make wise decisions. Instead, you'll become defeated, demoralised, and ultimately succumb to the righteousness of your negative inner voice and begin adopting these thought patterns as undeniable truths rather than cruel and overgeneralised subjective opinions.

One thing I've noticed over my years of life coaching is that no one ever considers themselves a 'closed-minded' person. It's not usually part of the list of faults people spiel off about themselves. You may consider yourself stupid or a 'loser', a failure who is lazy and fat, unlovable and unattractive, untalented, too shy, underconfident and passive, or overaggressive and impatient, but never closed-minded. You're a tolerant person, always open to new ideas, perspectives, and people. There's *no way* you'd ever judge someone inappropriately based on a societal label assigned to them; how they looked, acted, or behaved; their race, sexuality, gender, or career; their level of education; what tastes they had; their religious beliefs; or their political opinions...ah, that's a bit awkward. You do it all the time.

However, you cannot honestly call yourself an open-minded person 100 percent of the time. There will always be a political, social, cultural, or personal belief you are adamantly against and you will, on a conscious or subconscious level, judge those who subscribe to that belief, ritual, or culture. Whether you judge people for their diets, for having children, for believing in a religion, or for their beliefs about gender and sexuality, there will be people you are closed against viewing differently. You will generalise them all as being a certain way, believing in certain things, and always having a certain attitude and way of being. Whilst this is undeniably an illogical and unhelpful way of thinking, we're all guilty of falling into this mental pattern, and one of the most problematic ways you adopt this cognitive process is applying it to yourself.

To the same effect, most people are closed-minded about who they are, what their potential is, and how much power they have in the making of their lives and outcomes. People submit to the idea that they'll always be the way they are; the unfavourable circumstances they're in, behaviours, attitudes, habits, personality traits, emotional responses, and mental health issues are just who they are, and those will never change. They truly believe these things can't be changed. Your closed-mindedness towards yourself is what's holding you back in life. Your core beliefs that your genetics, disposition, health (physical or mental), status, wealth, personality, behaviour, circumstances, and location have an ultimate and overriding supremacy to overpower your autonomy and determine your potential in life are dangerously wrong.

Everyone has difficulties in life, some far more than others, but no one is fated to be a certain way or have a certain outcome in life. This disempowered way of thinking keeps people small, which is why people use disempowering words as a weapon. *You'll never be good enough. You're a failure. You'll never amount to anything in life. You're ugly. No one will ever love you.* These are horrible things some of us are subjected to in life by others and by ourselves. Some of us even use them against others.

> *Sticks and stones may break your bones but *words will never hurt you.*

(* Provided you have a strong sense of self which isn't dependent on external validation.)

It's easier to tear someone down to make them smaller than you than to put the effort into making yourself bigger and better, and it's easier to tear yourself down and tell yourself what you're not capable of than to try to be capable of something. Negative talk feeds into our negative biases, making them more believable, easier to digest, and acceptable as the 'truth.' The problem is that there is no 'truth' to your reality. There are only perceptions. You have a perception of yourself, and every other person around you has a different perception of you, and you will never make these perceptions align, no matter how much you try.

You're capable of achieving absolutely anything you set your mind to, and I'm here to make sure this book shows you how. But don't get it twisted. I'm not here to give you a bite-sized, easy-to-digest, ten-step programme for becoming more confident or successful. I can't give you that, and no one can, because no one knows where you're at in life other than you. Doing X, Y, and Z in that order may have helped me in life, but you may need to do Y, Z, X or even E, N, A! There's no manual to life, fulfilment, or success, nor is there a blueprint which everyone can follow without fail. We have to work a lot of stuff out for ourselves, and the main hurdle we need to overcome is the limitations we put on ourselves.

In this book, I'm going to help you unravel and remodel your thinking processes, core beliefs, perceptions, and behaviours by helping you understand the simple yet powerful psychological framework which has made you the way you are today. It's only through deconstructing ourselves that we are able to rebuild ourselves upon a more stable foundation of self-acceptance and go on to lead more empowered, autonomous, and significant lives. What I'm about to prove to you is that the art of personal mastery doesn't depend on your upbringing, past, circumstances, or personality but on your ability to manage your mind and challenge your beliefs, and your willingness to tackle life head-on.

CHAPTER ONE

THE EGO-TRAP OF SELF-IMPROVEMENT

I'M GOING TO HIT YOU WITH SOMETHING WHICH MAY make you defensive: you think you're better than some people. Admit it. No matter how low your self-esteem and self-worth are, there are people in your life, be they friends, strangers, colleagues, or relatives, who you think you're better than. Sure, there are people you feel inferior to—all those famous singers and actors, those gorgeous strangers on Instagram with fit bodies and glorious hair, your classmates who went on to live lives of prestige and riches, or your parents who you never lived up to. However, those of us who are more inclined to feel inferior to others due to crippling shame and self-hatred are more inclined to feel superior than those with confidence. Why? Because superiority is bred from an underlying inferiority complex. No truly confident or secure person ever feels superior to another, because their sense of self and worth isn't dependent upon a comparison. They had developed a self-sufficient validation system.

You may not be that arrogant person who parades their pride or belittles others for not meeting their standards (as one would expect from someone with narcissistic personality disorder), but if you're someone with an insecure sense of self and you struggle with low self-esteem, I can guarantee that you regularly compare yourself to others and feel fulfilled when you outmatch them. Knocking people down a few pegs, verbally or in the silent comfort of your own mind, is an easy but artificial and corrupt method for building yourself up.

Everyone with an inferiority complex has a shadow of a superiority complex buried inside them somewhere which reveals itself in different ways. Those with low self-esteem find themselves caught in the emotional chaos of the comparison flux: they feel amazing when they see someone doing worse than them in an area of life they're self-conscious about (such as their career or hobbies) but feel depressed and miserable when they see someone thriving in that area. For example, a person who is self-conscious about their weight may feel an unconscious or conscious sense of pride when they see someone slightly heavier than them passing them on the street, but feel immediately horrified and ashamed of themselves when someone much thinner than them passes. This is a shallow and unkind example to employ but, unfortunately, it's very common. The same goes for reunions with friends. People self-conscious about their career may not want to socialise with those richer and more successful than they are, opting instead to make friends with people they feel occupationally superior to.

People with low self-esteem waste away their evenings, mornings, lunchtime breaks, and lives comparing themselves to other people, and to make matters more painful, they're aware they're doing it. They're alarmingly aware of how bad they feel after spending hours online staring at photos of other people living lives they can only dream of, with partners they'd never be able to find, in bodies they'd kill to have. They promise they'll stop comparing themselves to others tomorrow; they unfollow the accounts which make them feel mediocre, unsuccessful, and ugly; they unfriend the friends and colleagues who make them feel small and decide to take up morning affirmations and positive self-talk. But then, after a few days, weeks, or maybe even a couple of months, they fall right back into comparing themselves to those 'better' than them. *'Why can't I stop comparing myself to others'?* They cry in frustration, *'It always makes me feel miserable'.*

Why then, I hear you ask, can't they stop? After all, they know it makes them feel miserable, and they have the desire and drive to make a positive change. The reason people are always unsuccessful in ceasing to compare themselves isn't due to a lack of will, determination, passion, or pain aversion. It's due to the incompleteness of their mission. Their apparent impulsive and inescapable addiction to comparing themselves to those 'better' than them isn't rooted in some subconscious, psychoanalytic masochistic drive; they aren't hardwired to seek data which fuels their self-destructive thoughts. No, they're only prone to negative self-comparison because they're addicted to positive self-comparison.

THE TRAP OF POSITIVE SELF-COMPARISON

When a person challenges themselves to stop comparing themselves to others, they only ever focus on cutting out negative self-comparison (i.e., against those who are superior). Nobody ever wants to give up positive self-comparison (i.e., against those who make them look good). People with low self-esteem are dependent upon positive self-comparison, which is why giving up negative self-comparison feels impossible. Their brain is hardwired to seek out those who are worse off than they are in some way, not out of malice or cruelty, but out of the desperate need to drown out their own toxic self-hatred. Both inferiority and superiority complexes are disempowered states of being. Both inadvertently depend upon other people to make the person feel special and worthy in some way.

Everyone wants to feel special and different from others, but they waste their energy, time, and life chasing a sense of significance through comparison. You can compare yourself to every single person on this planet and be none the wiser of your significance, originality, or distinctiveness. Even hypothetically speaking, if you were to discover by the end of your life that you were superior to the majority of people you ever met, in the grand scale of things, what would that even mean? What significance would such a status hold, and what positive meaning would it have to you or the world around you?

Nothing meaningful, impactful, or purposeful will ever come from self-comparison. You can be 'better' than all the people in a room, a stadium, or your life and still amount to absolutely nothing. The reason so many people are unfulfilled and miserable in life is that they take the well-trodden road of shallow materialism, one-upmanship, and empty goals for self-aggrandisement. They spend their time investing in self-serving ambitions with the intention of either bettering themselves or impressing other people.

THE EGO TRAP OF SELF-IMPROVEMENT

Whilst bettering yourself is a noble and admirable thing to

do (none of us can ever be totally selfless beings, nor should we strive to be, for our own well-being and security), many people strive to better themselves in limiting aspects of life. It's admirable to want to better your physique or become more academic, but dedicating the majority of your time to achieving your ideal body or to studying commits you to a limited field of interest and impact. You can manage your life in ways which allow your specialness to shine through projections such as *I am slimmer, I have more muscles, I have a better degree qualification, I have more followers on social media, I get paid more at work, I got another promotion*, but what else do you exist as?

All of these elements of self-betterment aren't innately harmful or bad, but the overemphasis of their importance leads to a life driven by the ego. There's no shame in loving fitness, education, your career, your mental well-being, or your health, provided they don't consume you and rob the world of who you are and what you have to offer. Very few people ask themselves what the greater purpose is for why they do what they do in life. Let's take a bodybuilder or fitness fanatic and ask them why they have dedicated their life to fitness. They will likely reply that they want to be fit to live a longer life, to which we must ask: a longer life for what? What do you intend to do with your long life other than continue training throughout it? Where do you intend to direct your energy other than to the weights and the treadmill?

They may reply that they want a long life to be able to spend more time with their family and see their children grow or to travel the world. Regardless of the answer, one must question them again and ask, *If that is your true purpose in life, what do you prioritise and spend more quality time with: your fitness or your children/friends/family?*

Whilst it may be hard to untangle (particularly if one is defensive about how they spend their time and what their priorities are), it's an important conversation to have with yourself. Why do you do what you do? Do you do it for yourself and the self-fulfilling results which only affect and impact you, or do you do it as part of a greater scheme and purpose, the priority of which is not you but other people and society as a whole?

I can see readers getting snarky at my remarks here, rolling their eyes at what they deem pedantic. *Who goes to the gym for a greater purpose?* Certain readers will scoff, *you can't assign meaning and purpose to everything. Self-care is essential in life.* True, but I'd like to retort with the notion that there's a difference between a person obsessed with the gym, who claims they want to live a long life but religiously spends most of their time in the gym, and someone who really loves fitness, spends a decent amount of time training professionally, but whose main passion in life is their social enterprise which focuses on supporting disabled athletes.

I don't mean to single out gym-goers and athletes, but they serve as a useful example. If your main goal in life is just to be fit and healthy, you'll find yourself living a life which centres and focuses on yourself and your needs, whereas if your main goal in life is to positively impact those around you by inspiring social, political, economic, cultural, or personal change, you will live a life with purpose, and everything you do will add meaning to that purpose, whether that is your diet, health, fitness, mental well-being, education, or socialisation. The tasks you build into your life for personal benefit should add more value to an ultimate goal which strives for external benefit and significance.

SHIFTING YOUR FOCUS TO A GREAT PURPOSE

Sounds a bit daunting, doesn't it? Most people don't think of their life in terms of external influence for the sake of the world around them, and that's understandable. We're evolutionarily hardwired to be primarily motivated by self-interest. On top of all that, life should be enjoyable and should include elements of self-care and occasional indulgences. Whilst personal interest and self-investment are valid and necessary pursuits in life, we shouldn't prioritise these above our pursuit of something bigger than ourselves, something which is capable of impacting our community and positively influences other people. Purposefulness in life comes through sharing what you have to offer with others, and you are too great an entity to keep yourself all to yourself.

The trouble is, how the hell is anyone supposed to identify their purpose in life or prioritise their goals without some divine intervention or eureka moment? It's not like we can just take a quiz on Google or a class in school to find out what we're supposed to do in life. There's so much noise in the world that it's nearly impossible to hear ourselves think. Everyone is drowning in a sea of chirpy-sounding notifications, over-scheduled calendars, mundane routines, pressing tasks, and avalanches of professional and personal projects, making it difficult for most people to focus on their most important goals and ambitions. Why would you want to spend your evenings and weekends after a long, laborious week at work researching how to set up your dream business when you could just relax your brain and scroll mindlessly through Instagram for five hours? Memes on Twitter are so much more entertaining than reading about taxes, LLC restrictions, and accountants. If you had to choose between watching four hours of an online accounting course, learning a language for an hour, or watching two hours of a new TV series, which one would you pick? Correction: which one *do* you pick?

Staying faithful to your priorities is hard enough when you're in structured, formal systems of education and employment, let alone when you're at home and dependent upon self-motivation alone. People spend their nine-to-five sitting at an office, feeling drained and bored to the point they sneak peeks at their phones during office hours to slyly log into Facebook when no one's looking. They check out the news during meetings or reply to a text under the table during a coffee catch-up with a friend.

Whilst you may lapse in commitment to your work or studies during periods of boredom, you still get your work done (albeit a little distractedly). Yet what about all those big aspirations you have in life, those major life-changing goals and projects you've harboured as a dream for years? The ones that don't pay you an hourly rate and don't fit into your nine-to-five or four-to-twelve working hours. You don't bother with them. You may commit to them for a month or so, but after you realise you're not getting any money for the time and energy you're exerting on them and there aren't any immediate consequences to not following through (like an angry boss or loss of income), you quit.

People always claim they don't have the time or money to do the things they really want to do in life, whether that's joining a night school to learn a new skill, eating healthier, exercising more, or reading more books. Sure, money can be an issue; it is for most people. But in most cases, when people say 'I don't have the money/time for X', what they're really saying is 'I don't want to sacrifice Y for X'. Life is about give and take, but people are creatures of comfort and habit. They don't want to sacrifice spending money on luxuries for six months, or a few years to save up for something like a startup investment or college course. Few people want to give up their relaxed evenings bingeing on YouTube or surfing the internet for hours in exchange for a few hours of reading or studying; nor would they want to give up drinking and going out in exchange for a healthier and fitter body or swap their Netflix subscription for a gym membership. Why? Because immediate pleasure is far more tempting and appetising than illusionary, distant, and uncertain fulfilment.

THE PROBLEM WITH THE PLEASURE PRINCIPLE

Our mental disposition to choose immediate gratification is referred to in psychology as the 'pleasure principle'. The pleasure principle, which is usually talked about in the realm of Freudian psychology, compels people to gratify their needs, wants, and urges quickly, whilst avoiding pain and discomfort. Needless to say, it has its place biologically; it's what drives us to breathe, eat, sleep, and drink when we need to. In other words, the pleasure principle makes sure we fulfil our essential and justifiable needs.

The problem with the pleasure principle is that it lacks parameters, meaning that it fails to keep us on the straight and narrow. Whilst, in theory, we should only crave things which are essential to our survival, our minds trick us into craving anything we want. We find ourselves needing alcohol, junk food, those new shoes, the latest gym gear, the newest phones, televisions, cars, and that latest designer bag everyone seems to have. People don't camp outside Apple stores days before the launch of a new phone because there are only a finite number of phones in the world and they'll suffer horrific consequences should they fail to secure the latest model. No, they do it because they feel an overwhelming need to have it first. This is merely an example of the pleasure principle working at its finest. It plays out according to a socially structured, superficial but all-too-psychological impulsive need to have something as soon as possible.

However, the pleasure principle doesn't always show up in such simplistic and easily definable ways. Take, for example, the concept of crash dieting. People crash diet because they want results quickly. Why slowly trim your calories by just 500 a day and lose a pound a week when you can slash them by 1,000 calories a day and lose over two pounds? Crash dieting isn't pleasurable; in fact, it makes people utterly miserable. They lose their ability to concentrate and they become irritable, deficient in certain nutrients, and potentially lose their hair. People know crash dieting is dangerous and, on some level, they know it can't be sustained, but the results are quick and the thrill of a noticeable change is addictive, so this becomes the route they take.

The pleasure principle in this example isn't obvious because people are consciously choosing a more painful and intense way of losing weight (i.e., becoming healthy by denying themselves food [in quantity and type] and adequate rest). There's little to no pleasure in eating dry salads; giving up all chocolate, carbs, and sweets; and substituting milk for water in your cereal whilst, on top of all that, going to the gym for three hours a day at 5 a.m. before work. However, according to their logic, being in the body they hate so much for a longer period of time than they have to is a worse fate than starving themselves and over-exercising for a shorter period of time.

In other words, being in their own skin is the pain they want to avoid. The pleasure lies in escaping it faster.

As you can see from the examples given, the pleasure principle interferes with our ability to have a realistic sense of timing and patience when it comes to nonessential needs, which is why most of us have seen (or been part of) mobs of people scrambling into stores during the Black Friday and Boxing Day sales. It also plays a major role in society's relatively new codependent relationship with social media. Contrary to the media narratives about the subject, our addiction to immediate gratification isn't just related to just social media—it's an evolutionary disposition. If we were to personify the dopamine molecule, it would take the form of Roald Dahl's Veruca Salt and would chant the motto 'don't care how I want it now' over and over again in a shrill but charmingly endearing voice.

YOUR INSTAGRAM ISN'T A MEANINGFUL INFLUENCE

We all experience the pleasure principle when it comes to social media in the form of digital notoriety. Beautifully edited photographs of your breakfast can garner thousands of followers and lead to sponsorship deals with McDonald's; what you wear to work can transform you into an inspirational fashion influencer; and your negative emotions, written out into brief but impactful statuses on Twitter, can make you into a trending and world-famous poet. Because social media platforms are built to translate your time into money, they structure themselves to feed into your pleasure principle needs, serving you tsunamis of perpetual instant gratification, validation, acceptance, and success. It's thanks to very cunning and clever businesspeople that you find yourself glued to your phone screen, endlessly refreshing your feeds to see if someone else has validated your post since the last time you checked. Who needs to work on self-worth, self-acceptance, and inner peace when you can work on building an audience online which will serve all the validation you need? Why strive to make a change in your community and work on something bigger than yourself in the world when you can get thousands of followers online and make an impact by sharing pretty pictures?

People throw years of their life into shallow social media posts under the false belief they're being impactful and adding meaning to the world, when in reality, all they're doing is adding more water into the ocean. You're probably thinking that I'm about to spiel off the benefits of deleting your social media and taking digital detoxes on a regular basis, but that's not the angle I want to take. Whilst evaluating your relationship and dependency on social media is a healthy and beneficial thing to do on a regular basis, the purpose of elaborating on the pleasure principle is to highlight why and how you're getting in your own way in life.

YOUR LIFE IS DIRECTED BY OPPORTUNITY COSTS

Your lack of progression and fulfilment in life isn't always about having low confidence or self-esteem (although those are huge factors, which I'll discuss in this book). Most of the time, your lack of progress boils down to your susceptibility to mindless biological instincts, such as the pleasure principle. Becoming mindful and aware of your innate tendency to choose pleasure and instant gratification over hard work and discomfort is the first step in the process of personal mastery.

You will never be completely mindful of all your innate urges, but becoming conscious about impediments in your life (such as the pleasure principle) and subsequently forcing yourself to become aware and take note of where they play out will allow you to manage your productiveness more effectively. Every time you choose to do something in life, you are choosing *not* to do something else. This is known as *opportunity cost*—when you choose to spend three hours a day on social media, you are choosing not to work on your project, yourself, your relationship, your business, or your skill. Opportunity costs are so influential over your life because they are intimidatingly unpredictable. The uncertainty of your future and the fear of living with the consequences of your decisions are enough to disturb your happiness, career, family, home, education, lifestyle, finances, and relationships. Should you marry that person and risk missing out on someone else with whom you have more chemistry? Do you quit the job which is making you utterly miserable and risk unemployment for an extensive period of time? Do you choose to never have children and risk regretting your decision in old age? Do you choose not to go to university and risk missing out on an experience you'll never be able to afford again?

Opportunity cost plays its part in all decisions, big and small. It's usually discussed by economists such as Tim Harford, author of *The Undercover Economist*, who gave a useful example of appreciating opportunity costs in his *Financial Times* column:

> Consider the following puzzle, a variant of which was set by Paul J Ferraro and Laura O Taylor to economists at a major academic conference back in 2005. Imagine that you have a free ticket (which you cannot resell) to see Radiohead performing. But, by a staggering coincidence, you could also go

to see Lady Gaga—there are tickets on sale for £40. You'd be willing to pay £50 to see Lady Gaga on any given night, and her concert is the best alternative to seeing Radiohead. Assume there are no other costs of seeing either gig. What is the opportunity cost of seeing Radiohead? (a) £0, (b) £10, (c) £40 or (d) £50.

Answer: Going to see Lady Gaga would cost £40 but you're willing to pay £50 anytime to see her; therefore the net benefit of seeing Gaga is £10. If you use your free Radiohead ticket instead, you're giving up that benefit, so the opportunity cost of seeing Radiohead is £10.

Let's give you another example. Say you go out for drinks with a friend, and your friend offers to pay. Even though your drink is free, you're still paying into the opportunity cost principle. Why? Well, because although you got a free drink, there's now an expectation for you to return the favour and buy them a drink in return. *But what if I couldn't afford to buy them a drink in return?* I hear you ask, *and my friend knew my financial situation which is why they insisted on paying.* The opportunity cost still exists, only now it has two forms: either (a) your friend doesn't expect you to be broke forever and will, therefore, expect on some unconscious level for you to buy them a drink in return one day, or (b) you pay an emotional cost in the form of the guilt you feel by not returning the favour.

But what if I wasn't a nice person? I hear you ask, *maybe I don't feel any guilt and I'm comfortable mooching off my friend.* No, even if you aren't a nice person, you still didn't get the drink for free. In order to get a drink, you had to pay the price of time and spend the evening with your friend. Even if you had no intention of paying them back and mooched off them for multiple free drinks (all of which you downed without a drop of guilt), you still exchanged one pleasure for another to be there. You spent the evening with your friend at the cost of spending your evening elsewhere in another enjoyable setting. You could have hung out with another friend, gone to see a movie, eaten some amazing takeaway food, gone to the theatre, or met some new people in an exciting new place where, unbeknownst to you, you would have met the most incredible person you've ever met in your life, who would have changed your whole world forever...that was the cost of spending the evening mooching off your friend.

Opportunity cost = What you are sacrificing / What you are gaining

CHAPTER TWO

WANTING TO CHANGE ISN'T ENOUGH

ONE OF MY GOALS OF THIS BOOK IS TO MAKE YOU REAL-
ise that you can do anything in life that you want to; but what
I need to stress is that whilst you can do anything, you can't
do *everything*. You can't be a professional dancer, illustra-
tor, entrepreneur of a multimillion-dollar company, famous
world-touring opera singer, skilled coder, championship
tennis player, and devoted family member at the same time,
ideally before the age of forty.

There are only so many hours in a day and years in life, meaning you can't do everything you want to the extent you would
like. You can try to do everything you want all at the same time
and become burnt out and exhausted, or you can allow the
opportunity cost to structure your life in a more effective and
productive way. Whilst you can't be all of those professions
listed above, you can experience them all in some way, should
you structure your life in a more efficient way. Opportunity
cost isn't your enemy. It's a tool you can use to structure your
goals and priorities in life to achieve all you want to, within

reason. This principle isn't about harshly restricting yourself or overthinking the sacrifices you need to make. It's about bringing awareness to the sacrifices and gains you make in life and weighing what the best outcome is for you at the phase of life you're currently in.

I once had a conversation with a woman I knew who sincerely thought she was going mad (for the purposes of this example, let's call her Elizabeth). She told me how desperately she wanted someone because her dream was to create and build a traditional family. Her methodology for fixing the solution, however, was interesting. She made it her mission each and every week to hit the town on the weekend with her work colleagues. She would spend each night flirting with some random guy she met at a club, who she would inevitably take home, sleep with, and never hear from again. Of course, there's nothing wrong with casual sex between two consenting adults, although an interesting social science study in 2008 revealed that there was often a link between casual encounters and feelings of regret, low self-esteem, and psychological distress, particularly in women.[1] Nevertheless, there was nothing wrong in this young woman's desire to hook up with someone in a club. The problem was that it wasn't the best method to get the results she wanted from the experience. The thought that she could only attract drunk men and that men only wanted her for sex depressed her, but she continued to engage in the same behaviour because it was getting her as close to her ideal result as possible.

She claimed she didn't understand why she did what she did. She started every Monday morning covered in unexplained

---

1   Elaine Eshbaugh and Gary Gute, 'Hookups and Sexual Regret Among College Women', *Journal of Social Psychology* 148 (2008): 77–89, DOI:10.3200/SOCP.148.1.77-90.

bruises and with her bank account a little worse for wear. She had no memories of the weekend just gone, besides the awkward, painful, hungover exchanges of the morning after, which left her feeling dirty and used for the rest of the week. She hated being drunk and feeling hungover, with all the nauseating emotions that came along with it, but nevertheless, she repeated the vicious cycle religiously. She would go out with the same people to the same club, drink the same drinks, dance the same dances, meet the same kinds of men, and have the same kind of sex. She really struggled to understand her own logic—why did she commit her time and energy to doing something that she hated over and over? She knew her alcohol consumption was turning her into someone she didn't like or respect; she didn't feel empowered or proud of herself. But she couldn't figure out why she didn't invest her time and energy into doing stuff she actually wanted to do, rather than wasting her life away in a toxic cycle which brought her misery and drained her bank account and emotional supply.

Her Friday- and Saturday-night alter ego was preventing her from developing and experiencing the kinds of meaningful relationships and lifestyle she genuinely wanted, but she found the idea of changing difficult and confusing. She wanted to do what was right for her, but she wasn't entirely sure what *was* right for her. Years ago, she thought what she was doing now was right for her, but now she found herself feeling unfulfilled and miserable. When you've spent years of your life committed to certain behaviours, routines, beliefs and habits, the idea of changing anything about them feels risky. This is because it threatens your sense of self and identity. Logically, you know how to change and what to change about your circumstances. In this case, Elizabeth knew she needed to do basic things like take a break from drinking (or going sober entirely), choose to spend weekend nights in or change where she went and who she went out with. The problem was that she, like most people, didn't want to change *enough*. She liked the idea of change, but she didn't want it badly enough to make herself change.

This dynamic of want and desire played out like a war in her mind—one part of Elizabeth wanted to become more mature and responsible, whilst the other part rebelled and scoffed at the idea and encouraged her to keep being herself and doing what she was doing. Elizabeth knew who she wanted to be and what she wanted to do, but she felt as though someone else was controlling and dictating her to stay as she was. She could feel her best intentions being purposely sabotaged by a power greater than herself, and no matter how much she wanted a better life for herself, she just couldn't make it a reality. Elizabeth felt broken, as though everything she did in life fell into ruin, and she began to believe that her will was much weaker than everyone else's. People told her to stop drinking and gambling, and she read books and magazines about how to be less destructive in relationships, but nothing could motivate her to take the advice she read or heard and put it into action.

You can read all the self-help books in the world; you can study psychology at university, attend courses, watch YouTube videos, and read article after article online about change, overcoming bad habits, altering beliefs, and overcoming things like depression and anxiety. But no amount of knowledge, education, or research will bring about the change in yourself that you wish to see. Learning about things is important, but learning only constitutes a fraction of the amount of work needed for change to happen.

People in Elizabeth's situation tend to become overwhelmed by the concept of change because they view the process as black and white. In Elizabeth's case, she knew she needed to cut down on drinking and going out, but she saw this as a major life change because she considered drinking and partying in all-or-nothing terms. When told to consider quitting drinking, Elizabeth saw this as a lifelong change, something which is daunting and overwhelming for most people. She didn't think of change in terms of short-term goals, like giving up drinking and going out for one weekend a month and then gradually increasing her sobriety to two or three weekends. Instead, she considered any withdrawal as a lifelong sacrifice which forbid her from ever drinking or partying again.

Of course, there are millions of cases where black-and-white change is necessary. People with serious eating disorders or drinking- and drug-related issues need to go to extreme lengths and go cold turkey for the rest of their lives to deal with certain habits, behaviours, and attitudes. As you can imagine, serious professional counselling and guidance are required for people in these extreme and dangerous circumstances because not only do they struggle with the physical withdrawal symptoms of their major life change, they also suffer from extreme versions of the same psychological issues most people do when they make big life changes.

Elizabeth, however, was in a fortunate enough position where this wasn't the case. She wasn't dependent on alcohol during the week and she didn't have a sex addiction; but because drinking, sex, and partying were such a huge part of her life and who she was, the idea of giving them up seemed self-destructive and threatening to her sense of self.

Changes which challenge us to alter our identity in some way are usually amplified and catastrophised in our minds because they're significant to us, even if the issue which needs changing is destructive. Many people with low self-esteem clutch onto negative and destructive behaviours because they lack a sense of self, so they define themselves by these negative traits that they've fallen into. Elizabeth didn't like that she was the party girl or the renowned hook-up chick of her friends' group; but if she wasn't those things, who was she? If she gave up partying and drinking, who would she be and what would she do? What would she talk about with people on Monday? Would her friends still like her and want to hang out with her if she wasn't the party girl?

THE FEAR OF LOSING ONESELF

The psychology underlying change and how people process it and handle it differently is too complex to summarise in a chapter. However, in cases like Elizabeth's (which aren't severe or potentially life-threatening), the reluctance to change is purely a fear of loss. Loss is a hugely difficult, emotional issue people have to deal with. People stay in unhappy long-term relationships and marriages because the separation from the other person would be more painful than the misery of living with them. Parents cry when their children go off to university or move out, and children break down after leaving their favourite toy on a bus. Because change always requires time, energy, effort, reduction, and elimination, people facing the concept of change equate it to a loss rather than a gain, thus leading them to procrastinate on instigating any kind of change.

Whatever your degree of confidence and self-esteem, the

organic cocktail of your pleasure principle and fear of loss creates a chemical baseline which fuels your procrastination. Whilst you may be able to identify your fear of failure or embarrassment as the psychological rationalisation behind your procrastination, what you're truly fighting against is your intrinsic desire for pleasure over pain. Even if you work on your fear of failure, your perfectionist tendencies, or your fear of judgment, your baseline, animalistic urge for pleasure and security will still impede your progress in life unless you become mindful of its prevalence in your behaviours and thought processes. So, whilst you may be more eager to focus on building your confidence and becoming some kick-arse guru than becoming mindful, the former relies on the latter. You can't master who and how you are in the world without becoming mindful of your innate lapses in judgment. Without mindfulness, we're susceptible to becoming passive spectators of life and, potentially, conceding victims of circumstance.

THE VICTIM MINDSET

Whilst we're on the topic, let's take a moment to talk about the victim mindset and how victimisation plays a huge, determinantal role in most people's identities. This is an extremely important discussion which I intend to handle delicately because I am aware *victim* has become a politically loaded word. So let me be up front. What I'm going to argue over the next few paragraphs is that the victim mindset is detrimental to your growth and self-mastery; it's something which doesn't benefit you because it holds you back in life and blinds you from your potential to grow, become more, and define your own life without external limitations. The victim mindset chains you to the belief that your past defines you; that your mental health, skills, personality, and habits are permanent;

and that the beliefs you adopted in your past due to your circumstances have more control over you than you do. The victim mindset tells you that you are powerless to determine and redirect your future or redefine your worth, and who you are today is who you will be forever.

Does that mean I believe victims are all weak and pathetic? No, they're people deserving of sympathy, love, care, understanding, and support to help them heal from their experiences and past. The only problem I have seen as a life coach is when clients incorporate their victim status into their present identity. Everyone has been a victim of something in their life, and the likelihood is that they will be a victim of something again. Some people go through horrific traumas whilst others go through less severe but more frequent traumas. Nobody goes through life untouched, and all experiences, good and bad, are valid, regardless of whether they are majorly life-changing, extremely traumatising, or mildly disturbing. I have met hundreds of people with traumatic childhoods, soldiers who have witnessed horrific deaths, people who have been harrowingly assaulted, people who were severely bullied at school, people who lost their parents, and people who spent years of their lives in emotionally or physically abusive relationships.

Whilst I'm very against the victim mindset, I'd like to distinguish my argument from those of extreme critics who discard victims and victim mindsets as insignificant impediments on social evolution. Unlike them, I don't deny the significance and reality of victims' experiences, the severity of trauma, and the complex psychological issues trauma breeds in people. Whilst I'm an advocate against adopting and maintaining victim mindsets, what good does it do to put people down who have a victim mindset? If others berate them yet offer no alternative outlook on life except *suck it up and get on with it*, people won't take their argument seriously and will just continue to perpetuate a mentality which is only harming themselves and their potential. My argument against the victim mindset focuses more on how harmful and detrimental it can be to your well-being and future potential when it is maintained in your present tense, and thus your present identity. As I will discuss in more detail in this book, your experiences in life constitute your worthiness to other people—who you become and how you allow all your experiences to mould you into a wiser and more empowered person transforms your intrinsic value. You may choose to disagree with me here, but I believe there's a powerful difference between saying 'I *am* a victim of X' versus saying 'I *was* a victim of X'.

I don't encourage people to deny what they've gone through or hide the difficulty they faced because of it. However, I encourage people to acknowledge traumas as something which *made you* who you are today, not *part* of who you are today. Whilst I accept that a lot of people will take issue with this argument, I would urge them to consider what benefits carrying their victim status in the present tense offers them. Does it empower or disempower them? Does it allow them emotional distance from the past or force them to carry it with them? Recovery is a long and difficult process, and no two people experience it the same way. However, I believe acknowledging it as something you've gone through rather than something you are living through is the healthier option. It doesn't take the pain away, but it helps maintain your autonomy and inability for the world to define you. Only you should define yourself.

Whilst it may feel comforting and easier to view your life

through a filter of *It's not my fault. They made me do it. It made me this way*, this submission to a state of powerlessness is not only debilitating but also smacks of immaturity. Whether or not you're conscious of your desires, the victim mentality is driven by two core needs: sympathy and vindication. Vindication allows the victim to renounce any responsibility for how their life unfolds, and the sympathy validates their feelings and emotions. When I talk about accepting responsibility in this context, I'm not promoting the idea of victim-blaming. That's a whole different argument which isn't deserving of legitimation. Unfolding the psychology of how people find themselves in certain situations and circumstances in life is a delicate process that varies from case to case. It is an important idea to address because understanding the limiting belief systems someone holds on to can help them uncover why they may find themselves in similar or cyclical circumstances, but this uncovering of patterns of behaviour isn't embedded in relaying fault or blame to anyone.

People with a victim mindset allow themselves to become governed by destructive patterns of thinking, behaviours, and attitudes because they have subscribed to the idea that they are not in control of their environments, actions, or emotional maturity. A person with a victim mentality who continually finds themselves in difficult circumstances with money, health, and relationships will feel as though the world is against them, that the universe is doing it to them and conspiring their downfall. They are quick to blame their boss, friends, parents, partner, children, pets, colleagues, classmates, or even God for the way things turn out. Victims are usually consumed by an unhealthy degree of anger, which is either internalised or externalised depending on their character. This unmanaged anger prevents them from acknowledging themselves as the common denominator throughout their recurring misfortunes. They adopt a passive role, and mentally and physically refuse to bounce back quickly after being knocked down.

People with a victim mentality aren't always easy to identify; whilst you have likely come across people who pull out the *woe is me* and *it's not my fault* cards quite openly, there are millions of stiff-upper-lip people who don't show any emotions and instead choose to internalise their self-pity and sense of victimisation. Yes, things happen to us. We can find ourselves in cycles of just bad luck. People do things to us, things take a turn for the worse, we find ourselves betrayed again and again, but we can't excuse our lives away based on past experiences and circumstances. People who take responsibility for their circumstances accept that bad things happen and situations can be difficult, distressing, and stressful at times, but they know they are responsible for finding a solution and implementing it.

YOUR BELIEFS DETERMINE YOUR WORTH

In his groundbreaking book *Man's Search for Meaning*, Viktor Frankl describes how he survived the Nazi death camps in Auschwitz, Germany. While many people might call him a victim of circumstance, Viktor defined freedom in a very intriguing way: 'To choose one's attitude in any given set of circumstances is to choose one's way in life'. Frankl elaborated further, claiming that 'between stimulus and response there is a space. In that space is our power to choose our response. In our response lies our growth and our freedom'.

Many people let their fear of failure, rejection, inadequacy, and loss run their lives. When left unchecked, these fears become deeply ingrained beliefs which render individuals helpless victims of circumstance who are incapable of making the changes necessary to produce positive outcomes. What many people with a victim mentality don't understand is that fear can serve them. It can help them break through their frustrations to achieve the outcomes they desire. Powerful people understand they have no choice but to try to succeed in life, because succumbing to fear only feeds disempowerment, stagnancy, and unfulfilment. For powerful people, the victim mindset is nothing more than an unnecessary chain holding them back from living exciting and rewarding lives.

You can have whatever beliefs you want about yourself and the world you live in, but beliefs and opinions are irrelevant unless you act on them. If your beliefs do not empower you and positively impact your everyday life and the lives of those around you, you'll never have any more meaning and purpose than someone who believes in nothing and does nothing with their life. Without having a vision for life, people perish. They waste their lives clinging to the past and allowing the weight of their regrets, mistakes, failures, and missed opportunities to hold them back from drawing up compelling life visions for themselves, filled with goals bigger than themselves. When our goals in life strive to positively influence and impact the lives of others, our confidence shifts. Whilst we may feel the pressure to ensure we fulfil our goals for the good of other people, our motivation becomes more powerful; we become more willing to take risks, lose face, fail, and make sacrifices for the good of the bigger picture.

Beliefs which don't move you forward, motivate you, or inspire you to grow and help others aren't useful; they're stagnating or regressive. This book will help you identify what beliefs you have and the role they're playing in your life (i.e., whether they're beneficial or detrimental to you). After reading this book, what you do with these beliefs is up to you and your judgment. You may deem them worthy of discarding entirely, or they may just need repositioning, adjusting, or modifying. Whatever you decide to do with your beliefs by the end of this book, you will be in a stronger position to compile a collection of beliefs which formulate a deeper and stronger relational foundation with yourself.

CHAPTER THREE

THE INCREDIBLE POWER OF BELIEFS

MOST PEOPLE ARE FAMILIAR WITH IMPOSTER SYNDROME; it's that sickening feeling you get when you feel like a fraud who doesn't belong and is on the brink of being caught and called out. Maybe you feel your promotion wasn't deserved or your status as a published writer was a fluke. Perhaps you don't believe you belong in the career you're in because everyone else seems so much more qualified and skilled than you, or maybe you don't believe you belong with the person you're with or the friends you have because you faked your way into gaining their affection. People suffering with imposter syndrome live on edge; they fear they will suddenly be humiliated and unmasked, as though someone lurking in their sphere of influence is taking notes and building up a collective folder of faults and inconsistencies to use against them one day. Whilst such paranoia is, generally speaking, unjustified, it doesn't help that we live in a callout culture in which people are eager to drag others' dirty laundry from the past into the public sphere at any opportunity in order to cancel that person and destroy their livelihood, reputation, relationships, and happiness.

People spend years of their lives battling with the difficult task of internalising their accomplishments due to feelings of illegitimacy. Whilst sitting in a big meeting at a job which feels way above their level of expertise, they're plagued with thoughts like *Do I really deserve this? I was just lucky. I wouldn't be here if x. I have no idea what I'm doing. I'm totally hopeless at this. I'm not qualified to be here*, etc. Before they know it, their imposter syndrome has gotten the better of them. It has stripped them of all self-assurance and merit and left them crippled with debilitating stress, anxiety, shame, depression, and low self-confidence. They begin to withdraw from taking risks, pursuing new opportunities, or striving to make a more meaningful impact with what they do.

Imposter syndrome is just one example of a type of insecurity many people feel. People can drown in chronic shame and anxiety over personal, economic, social, cultural, or professional insecurities. Because of the emotional pressure insecurities place on individuals, people are usually quick to find a solution to escape the discomfort and pain they're going through. The solution is usually somewhat dramatic: they crash-diet or starve themselves, change their appearance through surgery or extreme cosmetics, quit their job, cut people out of their life, delete social media, become more aggressive or more complacent and reserved, break off their relationships, or over-exercise. Whatever method they choose, the intention is to rip the insecurity from themselves in one clear swoop and disassociate from it entirely in the hopes that the problem will cease to exist.

What people fail to understand is that insecurities don't exist in the physical world. You can be insecure about physical and real-world things such as your income, weight, nose, breasts, arms, legs, career, voice, home, or opinions, but none of these things house your insecurity. They're merely things your insecurity is projected onto.

Thoughts are the mother of insecurities. Insecurity is nothing more than a thought, a belief, an ethereal object which cannot be dyed, slimmed, promoted, demoted, salaried, painted, broken up with, or bought. The worse you think about yourself, the worse you're going to feel in life. Your thoughts determine how you behave, act, and feel, and thus have the most critical impact on how you view and, ultimately, conduct yourself. Whilst people may say or do things which hurt you and feed into your negative beliefs, no one can make you think in a particular way about yourself; how you respond mentally and emotionally is up to you.

How you respond to moments of shame and insecurity reveals the process you undergo when externalising the manifestation of your internal thoughts. As your thoughts persist, so does your externalisation of them. The unhelpful and destructive behaviours your thoughts trip you into engaging with evolve into habits: turning to the bottle becomes your daily ritual, that cheat-day pizza and ice cream binge becomes your regular nightly dinner, your snappiness becomes your default setting, and your break from socialising becomes a state of permanent isolation. Before you know it, you find yourself in a permanent cycle of self-flagellation. You hate yourself for continuing to do what you do and beat yourself up horrendously over it, but no amount of self-chastisement is enough to put an end to it.

Your greatest problems in life aren't the actions you take, the emotions you have, or the things that happen to you; they're the thoughts you fail to manage. Your lack of self-discipline when it comes to accepting thoughts is the reason you find yourself acting in ways you wish you didn't, saying things you don't mean, or feeling emotions you wish you could get rid of. Nobody else can make you feel a certain way. They can't force-feed you an emotion to feel. They can do things and say things to you, but how you feel in response isn't their fault and isn't in their control. Your emotions are entirely under your influence due to the thoughts you do and do not validate.

RESPONDING VERSUS REACTING

You can't and shouldn't suppress your emotions, no matter how capable you are of monitoring and modifying your thoughts. Emotions are quick and, oftentimes, spontaneous. You can't always stop feeling how you feel, but you can always choose to manage your emotions through thought monitoring. The key to emotional management is learning the difference between reacting to your emotions and responding to them. Reactions are instantaneous, driven by unconsciousness and all that comes with it (beliefs, biases, and prejudices). Reactions serve as a defence mechanism: we scream when we're scared, we pull our hand away when we touch something hot, or we tense when we see something coming towards us too quickly. However, in today's world, where the evolutionary need for reactions has become less overt, reactions are things we associate more with regret and social interaction. There's likely been a time when you've said or done something without thinking because someone offended you or you didn't hear something correctly and jumped to a conclusion. You probably also regularly react to the news, comments online, videos, situations, and circumstances. Reactions are usually an all-or-nothing experience. You can react either super positively to something and feel elated throughout the rest of your day, or you can react negatively to something and find yourself feeling incredibly downtrodden and upset for hours, days, or weeks after.

Responses, however, are slow because they are not solely dependent upon your unconscious. They rely on the conscious mind as well. A response evolves out of a person's consideration for their feelings, the logic of the circumstances, the limitations of their perception of reality, and their core values (something which we discuss in chapter six). Responses consider the long-term effects they cause, whereas reactions don't take the future into consideration at all. Reactions are disempowering. They cause us to rely on biases, assumptions, fears, negative emotions, and limiting beliefs. Reactions ignite aspects of our psyche which don't serve us and are almost always antithetical to our core values. Emotions shouldn't be treated as an instruction manual but rather as a GPS. It's not in your best interest to follow and succumb to the instructions dictated by your emotions. Instead, use your emotions to unfold the internal root source of them to understand yourself and your emotional drives a little better.

YOUR BELIEFS CONTROL YOUR OUTCOMES IN LIFE

All of your negative self-talk comes from deep-rooted beliefs and assumptions you have made about yourself. Contrary to all the evidence you have supporting your beliefs, the majority of your beliefs are not only incorrect but unhelpful. Many people believe that life is a constant struggle, that they should always act nice and sweet to everyone, no matter how they're feeling. These people believe they are nothing unless they can prove their worth to someone and earn their love and acceptance. They believe their feelings are not important enough to be considered by others. They want to be loved and accepted so much that they bottle up their true thoughts and feelings to avoid all the confrontation and difficulty the thoughts and feelings may evoke.

Thoughts of being worthless and unimportant develop so insidiously over our lifetime that those of us who develop these mindsets never question them. We believe our worthlessness is a universal truth rather than a subjective opinion. Failing to acknowledge limiting beliefs as subjective opinions cause people to live stress- and anxiety-filled lives within the confines of a self-enforced enclosure. It doesn't matter if your teachers told you that you were stupid, your parents told you that you were worthless, or the kids at school all hated you and called you a loser. When you believe you don't deserve to have what you want, aren't worthy of anything better, or don't have the talent and skill to be taken seriously in life, it's not your teachers, parents, or childhood bullies who are making that your reality: you are. Your teachers, parents, or peers can't prevent you from living the life you want or achieving the things you dream of, even if all they ever did was put you down and grind your spirit deep into the dirt. People can say and do what they please to you, but they don't determine your outcome. How you handle them, what you take away from them, and what you choose to believe from them impacts your outcome.

When I was a child, my parents would always take my sister and me to the circus whenever it came to town. I really hated the circus; I found the clowns unfunny and the trapeze artists boring. This was back in the day when it was legal for circuses to have exotic animals, and I, like many children, loved seeing them. One year I noticed that the elephant in the ring remained calmly in place with nothing but a single rope tied around its neck, which was pegged into the ground. I couldn't understand why this most majestic, giant creature didn't just break free and run away. There was nothing stopping him besides a single piece of rope which he could easily yank from the ground with a small twist of his head. In my childhood, I was naive about the mistreatment of circus animals. It wasn't until I got older that I found out about how circus animals were rescued from exotic countries and sold to circus masters who then raised them up from their infanthood. Baby elephants were kept in captivity with just a rope around their neck, picketed to the ground. As a baby, an elephant isn't strong enough to free itself; it tries and tries with all its might until one day it gives up and admits defeat. The baby elephant believes it's not strong enough to break free, so it stops trying and carries this belief into adulthood. Whilst the baby elephant grows in height, weight, and strength, its mindset remains the same. We, as outsiders, know the elephant is more than capable of breaking free, but its belief system has determined otherwise, and so it lives its life the only way it believes it can.

As the elephant demonstrated, the only things holding you back in life are the beliefs you have about yourself. Most people don't like to admit they're wrong or accept that their perception of reality isn't helpful or accurate. People become attached to their beliefs because their identities are so tightly wound up in them. The fondness of familiarity sets people up for failure. Their goals get put on hold because they're burdened with limiting assumptions about their capabilities and potential. Their negative self-talk is what prevents them from going with the flow, taking risks, and making things happen. Overcoming limiting beliefs depends on a person's willingness to challenge and replace their beliefs with contrasting ones which feel uncomfortable, unfamiliar, and potentially threatening to their sense of self.

We aren't born with any beliefs. We're blank slates who take in the world around us and compose our thoughts in response to our environment and those who fill it. I must have been only around five years old when I entered my parents' bedroom one Saturday morning to find my dad still in bed. My dad used to work away most of the week so I was always excited when the weekend came around and I got the chance to see him and play. However, Dad was usually exhausted and in a lot of pain by the time he got home. Sometimes he had back pain and other times he had a migraine. On this particular Saturday, I ran into my dad's bedroom pretty loudly. Like many children, I wanted attention. I would fuss, play, and beg for him to get ready so we could go to the park. I was giggling, prodding, jumping, and running around the bed, eager for attention and affection in what I can only imagine was an incredibly irritating way when suddenly Dad responded. In a loud, solemn, and harsh voice, he barked a definitive no. I knew Dad loved me in his own way, but the damage was done early on. That small and probably insignificant incident stuck with me for the rest of my life. It was the first time I'd ever been rejected. I refused to accept the reality, so I persisted. I didn't want to grapple with the idea that my father didn't want to spend time with me, so I kept on asking him to take me out. This time, he didn't say anything. He just rolled onto his side, turned his back toward me, and farted.

My dad continued to reject me on Saturday mornings. What was once a one-off confusing incident became a patterned response, which left me questioning myself: if I was being rejected, what did that mean about me? I didn't have enough information to formulate a different response, and in general, children don't. They don't grasp the nuance of life and the different perspectives of a situation. They're left with raw data—my father rejected me; therefore, there must be something wrong with me. In school, there was a really pretty girl named Sandra. Her parents ran the local Chinese takeaway, and I thought she was amazing. When Valentine's Day rolled around, I used the pocket money I'd been saving up to buy Sandra a Valentine card and a Mars bar which I wrapped up in a bow. I found Sandra in the playground before school started, handed over my Valentine's gifts, and asked if she'd be my Valentine.

'Nah', Sandra replied curtly yet honestly. 'You stink.'

My child mind formed a pattern, a pattern which repeated itself both at home and, now, at school. Dad rejected me, and now Sandra had rejected me. For a child that meant only one thing: there's something wrong with me. I'm sure I'm not the only one who has experienced being the last one picked in a lineup for a sports team or has had to sit out of a game because they're the odd one out. No one takes the time to explain to a child that they're not the issue and, therefore, shouldn't internalise anxieties about their perceived inadequacies and imperfections. Whilst an argument for this reasoning may be that adults don't have these conversations because children don't have the intellectual capacity to understand such a complex psychological issue, people overlook this type of discussion with children completely, leaving them alone with their thoughts and early-stage negative bias development.

Children aren't taught the difference between thoughts, beliefs, opinions, and emotions. They assign beliefs to opinions (e.g., Sandra doesn't like me; therefore, I must be ugly and horrible) or thoughts to emotions (e.g., I think Dad hates me, and I feel rejected, unloved, and sad about this). Because no one teaches us the distinction between subjective, external influence and universal truth, we crystallise the negative beliefs we develop in childhood and carry them through to adulthood. We live in an endless cycle of stress, depression, anxiety, and beating ourselves up for being the way we are.

The negative biases we assign ourselves in childhood regarding who we are become our reference points in life. Throughout our adulthood, we naturally look for evidence supporting our negative biases. If your negative bias is skewed against your favour because you believe you're inherently wrong and not good enough, you will look for evidence to support and nurture your negative beliefs at every opportunity you get.

You are the negative constant plaguing your life. You are the one assigning meanings to experiences and parts of your life which eat you away and keep you up at night. You are the reason you stopped trying to apply for better jobs in favour of remaining in your dead-end, minimum-wage job for years. You're the reason you stopped dating because you believe that everyone you become attached to leaves you, and you're the reason why you started hiding who you are because other people in your life were ashamed of you, and you wanted to appease them more than yourself.

Beliefs act like a set of rules you're too frightened to break; rather than risk getting what you want in life, you'd rather remain in your comfort zone. Just like the baby elephant, you reach a stage in life where you stop trying to prove yourself wrong and, instead, continually look back at all the past events which support your limiting beliefs. You cannot continue the rest of your life speculating your future outcomes based on your past experiences.

YOU ARE GOOD ENOUGH

People waste their lives repeating the same few mantras to themselves over and over as they grow: I'm not good enough, I'm not smart enough, I'm not articulate enough, I'm not attractive enough, I am not, and never will be, enough. I didn't stop believing in my insignificance until I entered my thirties. Since my late childhood, I never thought I was good enough, and I ended up wasting the early years of my life trying to impress everyone else in the hopes that I'd be good enough for them.

Past failures, rejections, and losses don't reflect the conditioning of your life or foretell how you'll always be. Your past doesn't represent your capabilities or your value and worthiness. You are always good enough, but you won't always know the right strategies and techniques necessary to get the results you want the first time you try something. Just because you didn't know how to write an effective cover letter for a job when you were in your early twenties doesn't mean you won't have learned something by your late twenties or early thirties. Just because you didn't know how to handle the dynamic of your first marriage doesn't mean you didn't learn something to take into your second. You are not the sum of the mistakes you've made in life. You're not a failed employee, parent, spouse, child, or student, and you're not the embarrassing or stupid things you've said in moments of naivety or anger. The outcomes you get in life don't define you and shouldn't be part of your identity. Your value lies in your ups and your downs and the lessons you've learned from them all—failures and successes.

CHAPTER FOUR

DEFINING YOUR CORE BELIEFS

WE ALL POSSESS A COLLECTION OF CORE BELIEFS which determine our patterns of thought and behaviour. They affect the way we see the world, our habits, our ideas, expectations, prejudices and, ultimately, the way we operate in society and the outcomes we produce. You, along with most people, battle with thoughts and feelings which threaten to derail your success and happiness. You may avoid having intimate relationships or dating people because you have a core belief that everyone you love will leave you, or you may avoid going outside, looking people in the eye, or having your picture taken because you have the core belief that you are ugly. You may withhold trust and openness from people because your core belief is that most people in the world are bad and can't be trusted, or you may withhold what you have to offer because you believe everyone is selfish. These kinds of core beliefs will, obviously, have negative implications on you, despite their intention to keep you safe.

If you think everyone is better at their job than you are, you're less likely to take the risks necessary to impress your boss and get a promotion or be hired elsewhere; if you believe everyone you love will leave you, you may self-sabotage all the relationships you're in or avoid any kind of relationship entirely; and if you believe you're ugly and inarticulate, withholding yourself from speaking and making eye contact will cause you to become isolated and lonely because you'll fail to make any meaningful connections with people. Those who believe people are evil and selfish will become consumed by a prism of cynicism, passive-aggressiveness, and loneliness and may, ironically, become renowned by others for being selfish and withheld.

HOW BELIEFS WORK

Before we get too deep into this, it's probably best to start by asking ourselves: what are beliefs and how do they work? To understand how beliefs operate, think of how you use a computer. Whenever you need to copy and paste something on a computer, you have two options: you can either go all the way to the top bar of your screen and go through the menu item to select copy and paste individually, or you can use a shortcut via your keyboard of command C and command V. Beliefs are the shortcuts you take when navigating your way through life. They're your immediate and instinctual expectations of how the world will play out, but they're stored away in your brain within easy access in order for your brain to preserve energy when making decisions about processing particular types of data.

Having a pattern of beliefs for the brain to quickly resort to every time a similar experience or environment is crossed allows for efficient time- and energy-saving evaluations: less information needs to be taken in, digested, and processed. Of course, this has its pros and cons. Whilst, evolutionarily speaking, this rapid refining of complex data saves people a lot of time and energy, once your brain has a preference for a particular conclusion, it sticks to it. This is why you get trapped in negative thought cycles, assumptions, prejudices, and expectations. Your brain, even when provided with new information, refers to the same frameworks for guidance rather than constructing new ones.

Because you invest so heavily into the sensory evidence you intimately accumulate over your lifetime, it becomes difficult—in fact, nearly impossible—for you to disprove or reflect upon subjectively later in life. Beliefs form the majority of your self-conceptualisation, which is dangerous when you consider that the negative core beliefs many people have are always grossly overgeneralised and inaccurate. People believe they are failures because they've failed a few times in life, or they believe they're ugly because they've never been in a relationship, or feel unlovable because their parents rejected them. Even with gross amounts of evidence, none of these things can be true realistically. People like Thomas Edison went through thousands of failures, yet the failures never took away from his ultimate successes; beauty is in the eye of the beholder, and unless you meet every single person in the world, you can never categorically define yourself as objectively ugly; and whilst your parents may have rejected you, their love (or lack of it) isn't representative of the whole universe and all the people in it. There will be someone out there who will want to love you. Beliefs, good and bad, become problematic when people structure their lives around them. When your life revolves around your belief system, you'll find that any threat to those beliefs can leave you feeling personally attacked and invalidated (even if the challenge is for your own benefit).

THE FIXED AND GROWTH MINDSETS

But where do these core beliefs originate from? As mentioned earlier, they develop through your sensual perceptions of the world around you, that is, they're what you take from the messages you receive in life and how you fit within them. You pick up messages about yourself, other people, and the world through parents, friends, colleagues, teachers, news, events, experiences, and environments.

Let's take a look at an example of how some negative core beliefs can be developed. If your teacher wrote down on your report card when you were a child that you weren't good at reading, it was you who chose to believe their evaluation of you. From that point onwards, you acted out of the core belief that you aren't a good reader whenever you needed to read a book. Every time you opened a book, you would hear yourself say, *I'm not a good reader, why bother?* and you'd either read the book incredibly slowly or avoid reading it altogether. Contrary to popular belief, your teacher isn't responsible for your core belief that you're a bad reader, even if they didn't encourage you to get better. Only you are responsible for the core beliefs you develop. No one forces you to take on a belief and carry it for the rest of your life.

So, in the example given in the last paragraph, it's easy to blame a teacher for your developing the core belief that you aren't good at reading, but the teacher's subjective feedback doesn't equate to objective truth. So, an alternative way to respond to criticism could have been, 'OK, well I'm not good at reading *now*. I'll work on it until I get better', but most people don't respond to this method of criticism nor are they taught to. You were never taught to question, analyse, or challenge feedback when you were a child. Instead, you grew up in a culture where adults were always right, as were some of your peers (unless your parents convinced you otherwise). Everything you absorbed as a child, from parental disappointments to classmate teasing, impacted your hyper-influential brain. The younger you were when certain ideas about your intelligence, capabilities, appearance, and worth were imposed upon you, the more susceptible you would have been to adopt those beliefs in the form of a fixed state rather than a growth one.

Lewis and Virginia Eaton Professor of Psychology Carol Dweck theorised the growth-/fixed-mindset dichotomy in her book *Mindset: The New Psychology of Success*. The theory argues that those with a fixed mindset believe their traits, such as personality and intelligence, are deep-seated, unchangeable aspects of the self. Those with a fixed mindset, therefore, spend their lives trying to prove themselves rather than focusing on learning from the mistakes they made. In her book, Dweck writes:

> I've seen so many people with this one consuming goal of proving themselves—in the classroom, in their careers, and in their relationships. Every situation calls for a confirmation of their intelligence, personality, or character. Every situation is evaluated: Will I succeed or fail? Will I look smart or dumb? Will I be accepted or rejected? Will I feel like a winner or a loser?

Those with fixed mindsets, she argues, believe that certain people in life are dealt better hands when it comes to personality, intelligence, and charisma. They don't regard culturally admired and desired traits as cultivated skills people have developed through years of practice. Fixed-mindset people claim they weren't born to be a dancer, they're not a math person, they were built to be fat, they aren't naturally creative, or they weren't made for singing. Whilst there are those who are born with particular health conditions or disabilities which do hinder their capabilities with certain things in life, people who tend to utter these phrases aren't usually inhibited by such elements. They are merely making excuses to avoid practising, training, or starting something. This is, obviously, a dangerous pitfall for someone, as it impedes their skill development and growth, which, in turn, negatively impacts their health and mental well-being. It's only when people make the shift from a fixed to a growth mindset that they recognise the value of failure and difficulty and thus develop a passion for learning and pushing themselves out of their comfort zone and working through the trial and errors.

It's important to stress here that blame isn't the answer or solution. You can't shift your responsibility onto other people when it comes to addressing your core beliefs, no matter what roles other people played. If anything, you and your ego are to blame, but blame is such an unhelpful concept in itself that there's little to no use blaming yourself either. A better way of phrasing this idea is this: no one is to blame, and no one is at fault, but only one person is responsible for the beliefs you carry with you, and that person is you.

You invest in the core beliefs you carry with you, even if they were triggered by an external source. Whilst it doesn't help that your parents didn't encourage a growth mindset and maybe contributed to your inclination to adopt a fixed one, there's absolutely no use in blaming them. We're susceptible to adopting our parents' ways of thinking and being when we're young, but we aren't destined to maintain them. As we grow in autonomy and maturity, it is our responsibility to look at our thought patterns and behaviours and identify which ones are helping us and which ones are hurting us. Your ego is fully responsible for the core beliefs you carry: all the good ones and the ones which tell you that you aren't good enough or that you're broken, fragile, special, a failure, unattractive, or unintelligent. You can't pick and choose which beliefs you're willing to take responsibility for, and to place blame for certain core beliefs on other people is nothing but disempowering and unhelpful.

YOU ARE NOT YOUR TRAUMA

There are millions of adults who have overcome difficult, traumatic childhoods and the mental states these early life experiences left them, but there are also millions more who live lives of mental replay where they allow themselves to continuously relive the traumas, emotions, and thoughts that they produced. They hold on to the traumatic memories because they feel connected to them. Their traumas made them who they are today and, therefore, in their twisted way, the traumas are valuable to them. They believe that their traumas and struggles embody their sense of identity and self, but they come at the price of autonomy, productivity, and growth.

No one can amount to anything when they allow themselves to become trapped and defined by their past. Letting go of these memories doesn't take away what you've gone through or erase the legitimacy of your experiences. You shouldn't deny the things which made you who you are today, but they should exist as lessons, not memories. You can't use memory to power you on and you can't implement a memory to inspire others. You can only use the lessons you've learned from the memory to better yourself and the world around you. All other parts of hurtful memories are nothing but destructive and self-annihilating. You need to find the strength in what you've gone through and discard the rest. What you keep should become your core beliefs.

HOW DO YOU CHANGE CORE BELIEFS?

The question is: how do you change your core beliefs when they're so embedded in your sense of self? I understand that the idea of changing your beliefs can seem daunting, if not impossible. How can you undo a year's, a decade's, or a life-time's worth of conditioning? Whilst it may be challenging, it's much more achievable than many people would like to believe. You modify your beliefs multiple times throughout life; you are constantly outgrowing childhood beliefs and opinions and developing more adult ones. Dismantling your belief in Father Christmas and fairy tales is part of a natural process of growing up, and you spend your life perpetually constructing and deconstructing your beliefs.

You believed the boss at work hated you until you were proven otherwise, or you believed as a child that you hated tomatoes, but then, as an adult, you were proven wrong by your own taste buds. Some childhood beliefs are easier to hold on to than others. Whilst relinquishing your faith in the tooth fairy may come naturally, letting go of your deep-rooted belief that you were a mistake or that your father left you because he didn't love you is much harder to overthrow because such beliefs are embedded in a more complex field of reality.

When you believe in something, good or bad, you seek evidence to support and preserve it in your mind. If you've invested most of your life into believing you are a failure who will amount to nothing, that you're ugly with no hope of ever finding love, or that you're a horrible person who no one will be friends with, then no amount of evidence to the contrary will help you change your mind. You will always be biased towards your negative beliefs and unconsciously seek out every trace of validation you can find for them. You will be hypervigilant for every tone of voice which implies some-one doesn't like you, every potentially passive-aggressive dig, any insinuation of a backhanded compliment, every error you make, and every fault you can find in your persona.

Negativity bias is the reason why you dwell on insults and mistakes, flaws, imperfections, and upsetting memories. Due to the evolutionary nature of negativity bias, it develops in infancy after the age of one. Whilst it plays its role in keeping you safe by helping you keep more alert in potentially danger-ous situations, your innate inclination to be attracted more to negative than positive stimuli robs you of your ability to appre-ciate the joy you have felt in a day, month, year, or lifetime.

Negativity bias can have profound effects on not only your self-esteem but your relationships as well. Your biases can cause you to expect the worst in others or be more attuned to their faults and flaws. They can cause you to prejudge the intentions of or reactions from others, triggering you to act allusive, passive, confrontational, or avoidant pre-emptively, in order to avoid perceived negative outcomes. Research[1] conducted by Nobel Prize–winning researchers Kahneman and Tversky in 1984 demonstrated that negative bias can also hold you back from taking risks in life. They found that when

---

1   Daniel Kahneman and Amos Tversky, 'Choices, Values, and Frames', *American Psychologist* 39, no. 4 (1984): 341–350.

people weighed up the odds about a situation, they generally placed greater emphasis on bad outcomes than good ones. Even if the odds were fifty-fifty, the risk of loss had greater weight and significance than the chance of gain in people's minds. The research showed that even if someone hadn't gone through the negative experience before (and thus wasn't being controlled by negative association), their response to the idea of the negative outcome would still be stronger than the idea of the positive one.

So, how do you unlearn destructive beliefs when you're mentally wired to have a negative bias? The first step is to allow yourself to become open to believing in something new which conflicts with your existing belief. It's hard for people with low self-esteem to accept the fact that they have the capability and resources necessary to become the person they want to, but those flickers of validation they come across from time to time need to be noticed and recognised for what they are. You will have bad days, you will relapse into old habits, fail, or fall short of your expectations, but rather than allowing these negative experiences to feed and fatten your negative bias, you must hold at the forefront of your mind the following: *my old beliefs didn't serve me and believing in this will only keep me stuck where I am.*

You can't expect to change overnight, nor can you expect to eradicate the thoughts, feelings, and phrases you've used against yourself for so long. Whilst you may keep falling into the cycle of finding evidence for why you're a loser, a failure, a mistake, unlovable, or a bad person, your true aim is not to eradicate this language entirely but to instead repurpose it. Rather than accept the cruel things you call yourself as validation of your destructive beliefs, treat them as the subjective opinions they are (i.e., opinions grounded in years of psychological upset). These thoughts, whether they've been uttered or insinuated by others in the past or not, are your thoughts, so ask yourself: *What can I do to change my opinion of me? What do I have to change to convince myself I'm not what I think I am?*

You have spent most of your life trying to impress and change for other people: your bosses, parents, partners, children, friends, colleagues, teachers, and strangers. Yet you have rarely checked in on yourself and asked who *you* want to be, for yourself and others. People with low self-esteem are largely controlled and bound by self-hatred. This self-hatred not only holds them back in life, but it also puts a pause on them accomplishing things in life and making and maintaining meaningful and healthy relationships. Therefore, in the spirit of learning to live with yourself, you need to ask: *what can I do, say or think that will impress, please, and satisfy* **me***?*

CHALLENGING YOUR LIMITING BELIEFS

Identifying your limiting beliefs can be harder than you expect it to be. You may grasp the idea of *I hate myself*, but the reasons for this passionate, internalised aggression can be incredibly well hidden. There's an internal and external approach people can take to uncovering their limiting beliefs. The external process involves studying and documenting your actions and subsequent results on a daily basis for several weeks. Having your actions and consequences (be they emotional or physical) laid out in front of you as data will allow those of you who are more analytical in nature the opportunity to identify any patterns and dissect and explore the beliefs which may be causing them. The internal approach is better suited for those who enjoy methods such as meditation and mindfulness, as it involves just silently observing your thoughts and determining which ones you gravitate to and which ones appear most often. Again, both internal and external approaches benefit from using a journal as a tool for monitoring yourself.

After you've identified one or more limiting beliefs, the next step requires you to challenge and start doubting their legitimacy. Start poking holes in your beliefs by bombarding them with counter-evidence and arguments before finally implementing a replacement belief for them. Decide on what your new belief will be and start seeking situations and evidence which legitimise and validate the new belief. Even if you aren't fully invested in the new belief's validity, act as though it is true and cement your motivation for investing in it by imagining what your future will look like if it were true.

Over time, you'll be able to fully incorporate your new belief into your belief system and you'll learn how to identify and replace or modify beliefs accordingly as you go through life. The whole process takes a while and it's not a one-off solution. It's a continuous process which you will have to revisit and invest time and energy into over and over again. Whilst that may sound like a lot of work, it's much better than allowing yourself to accept a passive life which is stunted and depressed by limiting beliefs which rule your feelings, behaviours, passions, and endeavours.

There are two parts to changing one's beliefs. The first stage involves overcoming the fixed mindset and replacing it with a growth mindset, whilst the second stage involves replacing your limiting beliefs with new, liberating beliefs. The first stage requires self-defiance and rebellion. In order to become the person you aren't, you need to start doing the things you don't do. That seems easier said than done, I know, but small, repeated behaviours and actions are possible for everyone. Focus on the journey rather than the results. Don't focus on becoming a famous artist; just focus on joining an art class or online course and seeing it through to completion. Don't focus on losing one hundred pounds in weight or becoming a size eight; focus on completing a food journal for a few weeks, identifying your eating problems, and taking up some light exercise.

Most people go into change with their eyes set on the prize but become disheartened when that prize doesn't come to them as quickly as they'd hoped it would. They go in hard, buy new gym gear, join a fancy gym, bin all their junk food, and fill their cupboards with nothing but healthy food. Then, of course, the inevitable crash comes: the pressure gets too much; they went cold turkey too quickly and end up resenting their new lifestyle. They get frustrated that they're not seeing results fast enough and, before they know it, they quit entirely and resort to their old ways.

OVERCOMING THE FIXED MINDSET

The key to overcoming the fixed mindset is accepting that transformation doesn't happen quickly or easily. You will also have to tell yourself, firmly, that you are wrong and have been wrong for a long time. Despite what you've told yourself a billion times throughout your life, you are more than capable of being what you think you aren't and you have to prove yourself wrong with baby steps. You can't sit there in your room telling yourself that you're wrong, that you are in fact capable of becoming a brilliant writer, without sitting down and starting to write something. Losing weight, getting that job, achieving that degree, or acquiring that skill won't make you the person you want to become—the process of getting there will. Who you become along the way is what makes you evolve into the person you want to be, so stop defining yourself by your end goals and how close to or far away from them you are. Telling yourself you're capable is only a quarter of the battle; most of the battle revolves around defying yourself. Actions, after all, speak much louder than words.

Once you've started taking small but consistent action, it's time to start stage two, which involves identifying and challenging the limiting beliefs holding you back and impeding your progress. Identifying these beliefs becomes easier once you start taking proactive measures to defy yourself. You will find the voice becomes louder; in fact, it'll start screaming at you. Identifying what your core beliefs are will be difficult at the beginning because you'll be so accustomed to them that you'll consider these things facts rather than opinions. The questions you need to ask yourself during stage two are:

- What lies are you telling yourself / other people about who you are and what you're capable of?
- What negative traits about yourself are you holding on to rather than working through and with?
- What is it that, up until now, has held you back from giving your life 100 percent and getting yourself out there to do what you would absolutely love to do?
- What fears and beliefs about yourself and your abilities do you have which are holding you back from making an impact?
- What credible evidence do you have which supports your negative beliefs, and what evidence do you have to oppose them? How would your life be different if you stopped

being ruled by your negative bias and gave more weight and credibility to the opposing information than the confirming information?

- What idealised end goals are detracting your attention from the joy of the process? Challenge yourself to think of some examples when you gave up on something because your end goal wasn't being reached fast enough. Can you identify what limiting beliefs played a role in your decision to quit?

Once you've asked yourself these questions, list all your core beliefs and categorise them as either limiting or helpful. With your limiting core beliefs in front of you, extrapolate why they're unhelpful and then identify how you think they developed. You may not be able to identify their sources, but all the information you can extract from them during the self-examination process will help you in the future (as it can potentially save you from relapsing into old beliefs and thinking patterns).

The beauty of beliefs is that they can be unlearned; they're not chained to your psyche forever. Wanting to change, however, isn't enough; you can't out-think or outsmart your limiting core beliefs. All you can do is outdo them. Stop complaining, stop submitting, stop wallowing, and start taking action which defies everything you believe in. Then, watch your whole world shift.

CHAPTER FIVE

GEORGE MICHAEL WAS RIGHT

IN 1986, BIG-HAIRED, SMOOTH, AND HANDSOME EIGHT-
ies pop idol George Michael came to the realisation that he had
been living inauthentically. Whilst he'd achieved incredible
notoriety and success alongside his *Wham!* bandmate Andrew
Ridgeley over the previous five years, his future felt elusive.
Pop music was unstable and the dynamics of his band weren't
as strong as they had once been. By the age of twenty-three,
he found himself alone, solo, and depressed. He felt his time
in *Wham!* had left him misunderstood and misrepresented as
an individual and as an artist, which is why, in 1987, George
returned with a whole new look and rock-and-roll pastiche
with his debut solo album, *Faith*. George explained that the
song 'Faith' represented the way he felt at this time in his life:
'It's kind of another word for my hope and optimism. You know,
faith to me is just really such a strong word and the more I got
into the idea of the song being the single, the more I liked the
idea of using it as the title track.'

For those who aren't religious in any way, *faith* can seem
like an uncomfortable word to use. Its significance is deeply
entrenched in religious connotations, which makes the word

taboo to many people. However, George Michael (who wasn't religious, despite attending a Christian school) was right: you gotta have faith. Fundamentally, the word *faith* has nothing to do with spirituality, despite being adopted by all sects of spirituality. Faith means having complete trust and confidence in somebody or something, and it's likely that you already use the term *faith*, regardless of your religious inclination. You've probably expressed in the past that you've lost all faith in humanity, have no faith in politicians, or have little faith for the future of our planet. You expect your partner to be faithful; you scour the internet for adorable stories about kittens being saved by strangers to restore your faith in humanity, and you've spent years of your life dropping in and out of faith that you'll achieve everything you'd dreamt of.

Yet you rarely apply faith where you need it most: in yourself and your future. People with low self-esteem and low confidence have little to no faith in their ability to turn their lives around; they have no faith in their potential or their prospects. Their lack of faith prevents them from putting themselves out there to pursue their goals and visions; it makes them pessimistic and afraid and, therefore, more inclined to live a conservative and reserved life.

MARGARET'S BIRD

I've told most people in my life the allegorical story of Margaret's bird. This wee bird lived in a beautiful fishing village called Portsoy up in the north of Scotland with Margaret, an elderly spinster whose only company in life was her little budgie. Margaret kept her wee budgie in a decked-out birdcage in her living room during the winter months; he had all the mirrors and trinkets he could ever want and loved flying around the living room whenever Margaret let him stretch his wings. In the summer, however, Margaret moved the birdcage to the kitchen, which had much nicer lighting and views of the sea and sun for her little bird to enjoy. Margaret thought she was spoiling her small friend when, in actuality, these months were torture to him. He lived a life of blissful ignorance for nine months a year, but when summer rolled around, he got to see everything he was missing: the warm sun, salty winds, crisp sea waves and, of course, other birds. He was never more aware of his cage than when he sat there, trapped, watching the other birds swoop past the window and dance with each other in the trees and pitter-patter across the lawn.

One beautiful sunny day, Margaret decided she would spend a long day at the beach reading. She packed up her bags, opened the cage to let her little bird fly around whilst she was gone, and left her home, foolishly leaving her kitchen window open. The little bird hopped down onto the ledge of his birdcage and looked longingly at the open window. This was his chance for freedom, once and for all. He could finally find out what wind felt like; he could eat berries all day long, bathe in puddles, and hop around in the dirt to dig for worms. Perhaps, he thought, he could even try to build himself a nest and find himself a little girlfriend to start a family with. Then doubt and fear crept into his mind. What if none of the other birds liked him, or what if some of these birds were dangerous? If there were birds, there were surely other beasts out there which could harm or even kill him should they want to. What if he couldn't find any berries or worms, or build his own nest? How would he survive? Then finally, he thought, what about poor Margaret? She'd spent years treating him so kindly and she didn't have anyone else in her life. Surely she'd be so lonely and upset.

The little bird spent hours procrastinating, contemplating all the pros and cons of freedom. He wanted his freedom, but he was terrified of leaving the security and comforts he had. He was so lost in his thoughts that he hadn't even noticed the sky had turned dark outside, nor had he heard Margaret enter the room. It was only when he heard a shriek and the slam of the window closing that he became aware of his surroundings. Margaret, relieved, tickled her little bird's chest and cooed affectionately as she locked his little birdcage and draped a blanket over him. With a sigh of defeat, the little bird ruffled up into a huddled ball, accepted his fate, and fell asleep.

FEAR IS A LIFESTYLE CHOICE

You want to be free: free to express yourself, to do the things you enjoy, and to make a difference in the world in some way. You don't want to live an insignificant life where you waste away in a dead-end job which means nothing to you; you want to live an exciting life full of enjoyment, passion, and vigour. But what's holding you back? The same thing that kept Margaret's bird from flying out the window and living the life he had only ever dreamed of: fear. Margaret's bird wanted freedom, but his worst enemy (his critical voice) struck him cold with doubt. He became plagued with images of worst-case scenarios. He kept asking himself what would happen if he wasn't good or skilled enough, or what would happen if he didn't get what he wanted.

Fear is the primary reason why you aren't where you want to be in life. You're crippled by it. For many people, having a positive vision for the future is equally exciting and terrifying. You've likely been beaten down in life, which has left you feeling doubtful and cautious about what you do and how you approach every aspect of life. You limit yourself to safe spaces, things, people, habits, environments, careers, and challenges. Margaret's bird daydreamed about freedom every summer: he was curious, excited, and passionate about his future potential and possibilities, yet he chose comfort over freedom because his fear of the future outweighed his faith in himself. Why? Because he wasn't secure in himself.

People with low self-esteem are insecure with every aspect of themselves and who they are; but you will never be capable of expressing yourself freely in life until you become secure in who you are. Margaret's bird wanted security over freedom, and I relate to him. For years of my life, I chose job security, social groups, people-pleasing, and social climbing in order to get ahead in life. I found out the hard way that compromising my own integrity and standards to fit in with other people was imprisoning rather than liberating. Margaret's bird, like people with low self-esteem and low confidence, valued the security of their external environments because they lacked a secure internal environment. Someone who is fundamentally secure in who they are is already free because they don't need to rely on external factors for security. Their security is internal, so no matter where they go or what risks they take, they know they carry their secure foundations with them. You can chase money, relationships, validation, friends, fame, success, and popularity, but no amount of money can buy inner tranquillity and self-acceptance. You will never be free from judgment until you stop caring what people think, you will never be financially free until you stop chasing materialism, and you will never be free from the life which makes you unhappy until you take responsibility for it.

Fear is a lifestyle choice people commit to. It would have been easy for Margaret's bird to step out of the cage and fly away, but he didn't because he chose not to. The opposite of living a life in fear is living a life in faith and, no, not spiritual faith (although you can add a spiritual faith to your lifestyle should you want to). I'm talking about the faith George Michael sang about: the faith in the self. The faith that everything will turn out alright, notwithstanding trials and tribulations, because you are capable of making things work out because you have enough faith in yourself to persevere. This faith isn't spiritual or psychological—it's proactive. You don't think in faith; you act, behave, and react in faith (the phrase, after all, is taking a *leap* of faith, not making a mental note of faith). Acting in faith, however, is a two-part equation. Those who have faith in themselves to get through the worst, handle hardships, and develop the skills they need to grow also have something else: a willingness to take a risk. Risk and faith are symbiotic: they cannot exist effectively without each other. Risk is required for change to take place, and faith is necessary to free yourself from being controlled by fear.

THE BEAUTY OF TAKING RISKS

A single incident in my early twenties made me aware of the dichotomy between faith and fear. I was living in Australia at the time, backpacking up the West Coast to Darwin by myself. Because of Australia's chilled and friendly culture, I was regularly picking up backpackers for company. One day, I picked up three guys who had all found each other whilst backpacking: one was a native Australian, whilst the others were from New Zealand and Germany. In the early hours of the morning, the guy from New Zealand ran into our room to announce that he'd bagged us a boat with a glass bottom. He'd heard that the giant turtles had recently had their babies and thought it would be the perfect opportunity for all of us to sail out and go scuba diving to try to catch a glimpse of them.

It was a once-in-a-lifetime opportunity, so even though we were all shattered, we packed our wetsuits and dashed out to sea in the early hours. Once we were far enough out to sea, we dived in. All of us were experienced divers, so we scattered slightly in the sea. I fell behind because I was taking pictures with my dodgy underwater disposable camera. I had become enchanted by all the soulful colours of the fish and coral and was swimming in blissful tranquillity until, suddenly, I saw a shadow flash right underneath me. My heart sank to the pit of my stomach. I knew precisely what that shadow was. In a moment of panic, I debated whether or not I should swim back and save myself or swim ahead to catch up with the others and warn them. Of course, I swam on and rounded the others up to the surface to break the bad news. There was a big bull shark nearby. The Australian, being far braver, dived again and returned to inform us that we were, in fact, being circled by two bull sharks.

I'd never felt so lost and helpless. I'd served in the army for years, but unlike in the army, here I wasn't armed, trained, or prepared for this danger. It was just me and the brute and unforgiving force of nature. We all turned our attention to the New Zealander, who had been very openly religious. For some reason, it felt appropriate that he say something in our time of need. The pressure the poor guy must have been under cannot be imagined, but with a stammer, he took the lead. He said a few words of prayer where he asked for the sharks to be distracted by another source of food. It was simple and somewhat naive in nature, but during that moment I felt hope. I've had a strange relationship with religion my whole life, and it's not something I'm sure about to this day, but it wasn't the idea of a god which comforted me at that moment. The prayer gave me the faith of an alternative outcome. What if the sharks did just leave? What if they did find another source of food which wasn't us? In my moment of fear and panic, I hadn't thought of any alternative options other than immediate death, whereas now, the idea came into my mind that survival could be an option.

What's more, the prayer made me realise how little control I had in my current situation. Whilst most people find the idea of losing control anxiety-inducing, my awareness of my powerlessness made me feel at peace. Why should I worry about something I couldn't control? It wasn't in my hands or anyone's hands; it was just down to luck and circumstance. My panic faded and diluted into a peacefulness, as seemed to happen with everyone else. The Australian decided to lay out our reality, deducing that there were four possible outcomes: we could either swim back to the boat and get attacked by the sharks, swim back to the boat and not get attacked, swim out to see the turtles and get attacked on our way back, or swim to the turtles and get back to the boat without getting attacked. We had a 50 percent chance of getting attacked; the question was: did we want to risk seeing the turtles or not? Those turtles could potentially be the last things we saw, but would we feel more at peace with completing our mission to see them than not trying at all? We decided that we'd come this far already and we might as well try to see them.

They were utterly beautiful. They were worth every ounce of fear we felt that day. It was truly a once-in-a-lifetime opportunity. As you have probably deduced from this tale, we made it back to the boat without getting attacked; the only problem was that our motor packed in when we were around twenty yards away from the shore. The story ends with a group of stressed, frustrated, but still nervous young men jumping from the side of the boat and swimming with their dear lives towards the shore, upon which they collapsed. I'm not saying that we survived due to some divine intervention, because that's not what I believe happened. What I am saying is that the prayer moment gave me time to pause, which my panic and fear wouldn't have granted me. That pause gave me the chance to switch from living in fear to living in faith: faith that I could survive this, faith that there was another option other than death, faith that I was strong enough to see it through to the end. Living in faith doesn't require a belief in God or spirituality: it only requires you to stop living with an expectation of the worst-case scenario. Living in faith means reacting out of peace rather than anxiety, panic, stress, tension, and chaos—it doesn't require divine intervention.

Acting in faith involves accepting that you cannot control the things which happen to you. Yes, you can influence your future through the decisions you make, but you have no control over how things unfold and what happens to you. You can't control how other people treat you, the economy, politics, all aspects of your health, or the interactions you have. All you're able to control in life is how you respond to what happens to you. This can sound like an alien and potentially impossible idea to those who have lived their life caught in what feels like a perpetual whirlwind of chaos and drama, but you are always in control of how you view and digest life circumstances. Life should be lived inside out, not outside in. When you allow your emotional and mental well-being to be controlled or manipulated by your unmonitored thoughts, external circumstances, or forces, you become immediately disempowered and out of control. Proactive and confident people, however, will always choose to rise above their circumstances by responding to them in a way which encourages and promotes personal development and growth. They don't allow life to redirect them and carry them away entirely. They take full control of their outcomes despite the fluctuating and unpredictable world around them. I'll go into more depth about how to choose your responses in chapter twenty but for now, all you need to focus on is letting go of the reins. Accepting that you have no control over what happens to you will allow you to develop a more positive and peaceful mindset. This may seem like a naive approach to life to some readers, but it's a far more effective approach to life than one which is dominated by anxiety, fear, and worry.

CHAPTER SIX

VALUES: YOUR DRIVING FORCE

UNDERSTANDING WHO YOU ARE IS A LIFETIME PROCESS, and most of that process involves unfolding and exploring your personal philosophies and values. Core values are the fundamental principles you live by and measure your standard of living against. Your behaviours, thoughts, and emotional investments are guided by your core values. In fact, the only reason you're here, reading this book, is because you've acted in accordance with your core values. Whilst there will have been moments in your life when you've consciously adopted a new value (perhaps because a book or documentary enlightened you about ethical standards of a global or social issue), most of your values were developed subconsciously and unconsciously. You developed your core values through your life experiences, events, familial and peer opinions, social conditioning, and media consumption.

But before we get too deep into the topic, I should first clarify the difference between core values and core beliefs. Core beliefs develop around your values; they are the unquestioned convictions you accept as true, based on limited, biased, or nonexistent evidence. Core values, on the other hand, are the aspects of life you deem to be important, from personality traits to ways of living, ethics, education, or equality. Your values determine what drives you, which means taking the time to understand your values will help you discover what your passions and motivations are in life.

Due to the nature of personal development, core values are usually impressed upon you by your guardians in early childhood. Of course, not all of your core values are positive. Unfortunately, being exposed to the harsh realities and circumstances, such as uncertainty and fear, early in life means you're more predisposed to developing negative core values. So, whilst you may have been taught to value honesty, you may also have been taught to value personal wealth and material consumption to an unhealthy degree; and whilst you may have been taught to value compassion, you may have also been taught to value self-doubt and regard self-deprecation as a symbol of genuine humility.

HAPPINESS VERSUS FULFILMENT

I once had a conversation with a young man who really valued work, money, and success. All he wanted in life was to be successful but, like everyone, he had his own definition of what success meant. When I asked him what got him out of bed every morning, he told me it was work. He loved working because he loved the buzz he got from making commissions and securing bigger and better deals. Making money, he told me, was what excited him more than anything.

Naturally, I was curious, and I leant into the subject, asking him what he thought the purpose of making money was. He told me the purpose of making money was to be able to buy a new house and buy nice things like a flashy car or another holiday. Again, I challenged the purposefulness of all this: what was the purpose of getting a new car or a new house, or going on holiday again. His answers became slower in delivery; he began discussing the practicalities of being a homeowner, the fun of going on holiday, and the efficiency of getting a new car to get to and from work with. Ultimately, he concluded, the purpose of these things was to make him happier and more comfortable.

'You may be happy, but are you fulfilled?' I asked him. The young man tipped his head in confusion before laughing off the idea: 'No way, I don't have enough yet. But when I've gotten further in my career and can afford the lifestyle I want, I definitely will be.'

It's easy for you and me to hear this story and scoff at the blatant lack of self-awareness, but realistically, do any of us truly know when enough is enough? When it comes to chasing the things which make us happy, such as careers, money, clothes, or holidays, are we really confident that we'll know when we have enough to make us feel truly and completely fulfilled? You can keep getting promoted, move to a new house, and upgrade your life and the things in it, but can you honestly call these things fulfilling? Particularly considering you could lose your home, crash your car, or get fired from your job any day.

There's a significant distinction between happiness and fulfilment, which I will elaborate on later in this book, but the point I'd like to make now is that this young man wasn't aware, as many people aren't, that buying or attaining happiness doesn't lead to fulfilment. He could choose to live the life of luxury and leisure, he could work all hours of the day to earn more and more money and take as many holidays as his heart desired, but at what cost? I asked him whether or not he had much of a social life, whether he spent much time with his family and friends, and he said no, he didn't have the time to.

Relationships are one of the first things people sacrifice in the pursuit of 'happiness'. They forget the significance of connection and totally overlook how important a sense of belonging is to one's self-worth and value. Think back to the last time you went on that holiday you saved years for; that holiday you told everyone about and spent your office hours daydreaming of in anticipation. If you were to ask yourself what the most fulfilling part of your holiday was, would you argue it was the poolside you spent hours sunbathing on or the wonderful locals you met and connected with, or the moments you shared with your family and friends?

This young man is not an anomaly: millions of people become addicted to the pursuit of significance. Personal significance, to them, is a core value, so they do everything in their power to prove their worthiness to other people. They work through the ranks, achieve greater statuses, buy more expensive things, and win more awards. Like most people, I spent years of my life chasing titles of significance in the hopes that I would drown out the booming internal narrative reminding me of my own insignificance. I was so insecure of who I was that I joined the army. No, that doesn't mean everyone who joins the army is trying to outrun an internal feeling of insignificance, but in my case, I was. I saw soldiers as macho heroes who automatically earned respect and adoration due to their bravery, skill, and strength, so I wanted to be one. I believed that being a soldier was enough; all I had to do was achieve that title, maybe climb a few ranks, and then boom, I'd be forever significant, and no one could take that away from me.

LESSONS FROM A MOVIEGOER

One of the biggest wake-up calls I had to the emptiness of significance took place in a Dundee supermarket (you'll find over the course of this book that the most enlightening moments tend to show up in the least poetic places). I had just popped in for a sandwich, pretzels, and a coffee on a lunch break; I'd been in workshops all morning and was ravenous, arguably on the edge of being 'hangry'. As I turned the corner on one of the aisles, I passed a man with a trolley full of nothing but Coca-Cola and pretzels, the exact same pretzels I had in my hand. Being a chatty guy, I made a passing remark on his excellent choice of pretzels, only that passing remark turned into my downfall. I suddenly became trapped in what felt (in my starved and frustrated state) like an hour-long, in-depth monologue with a stranger in a supermarket. This chap saw his opportunity to talk to someone and latched on with a grasp so tight it was as if he had grabbed time by the ankles and held it hostage. The pretzels and cola, he told me, were cinema snacks. He was part of a cinema membership scheme where he paid monthly for unlimited access to all film screenings at his local cinema, and this was his weekly snack shop.

I'm sure you've been in a situation where you're painfully disinterested in what someone is talking to you about yet are hyper-conscious about not wanting to come across as a rude arse and offend them. So you end up politely standing and nodding whilst simultaneously giving social hints through your body language that you would rather push pins into your eyes than be stuck here. Unfortunately, my cues were not picked up. He told me all about the films he'd watched recently, going into depth about their plots, his reviews of them, and the controversy his opinions sometimes stirred up. He was apparently part of a nationwide online forum of cinema membership members who shared their film reviews amongst themselves. According to this forum, this man who I was talking to was the unrivalled number-one member on the leaderboard. That meant that he'd gone to the cinema more times than anyone else in the country. I could tell by the way he talked how incredibly proud he was of his title; he spoke of it as though it were his greatest accomplishment. My inner monologue, fuelled by ravenous hunger, was not so complimentary. Completely disinterested in his monologue, I began rolling my eyes, wishing this sad man would just get a life and leave me alone. It wasn't until I took a moment to listen to myself and register my unkindness that I consciously quietened my mind so that I could try to hear what he was *actually* saying to me.

He wasn't telling me about the films he loved to encourage me to go see them myself, nor was he encouraging me to join the membership scheme. This conversation only had one message: *I am number one. I am the top-ranking cinemagoer in the United Kingdom.* In other words: *I am significant.* From what I could gather from his dialogue, his two- to three-times-a-day cinema visits weren't an overt boasting of laziness; it was his routine, the only security and rhythm he seemingly had. His forum wasn't a meaningless online space; that was his family and friends. This guy clearly didn't take any risks in life. He went to the same cinema and took the same snacks and talked to the same people every day for years and years. As I listened to him talk, I couldn't help but wonder what progress and growth he was making in life; everything he did seemed cyclical. Was this truly fulfilling to him; did it really drive him to get out of bed every day?

People are more obsessed with labels and status than they realise. In fact, most people put status above genuine personality. A prime example of this is the global infatuation with fame and celebrity. People idolise and wish they were friends with famous singers, actors, and celebrities just because they've seen them on a show, read a few interviews with them, and maybe met them briefly after a gig or on a red carpet. They've never spoken to them before, hung out for coffee, or even spent more than a minute of their lives getting to know them in person. Yet they still love them unconditionally, adore everything they produce, and get excited at the thought of bumping into them or seeing them live one day. Conversely, they would never dream of going up to a stranger who they've never spoken to or introduced themselves to and ask them for a hug or autograph. They may have seen the same barista in a coffee shop and loved every coffee he's ever produced for them, but they'd never dare tell him how much they love him and his work in a nervous, giddy voice. They'd never collect photographs for their bedroom wall or Pinterest board of a stranger they passed every day because they liked their style and thought the person was handsome or beautiful. Well, they wouldn't unless they wanted to get arrested.

There's a logical reason why people don't scream with excitement, jump up and down, take out their cameras, and ask for a selfie when they see strangers: it's because they lack the status of a celebrity. The strangers you pass on a daily basis may, in their own private lives, be talented musicians, actors, or wealthy multimillionaires, but because they lack status and significance to the general passerby, nobody cares about them. People want a selfie with a celebrity or want to become friends with a celebrity because of what *they'd* get from it. They don't care about who the celebrity is as a person (although they *think* they do, based on their intensely limited and PR-marketed knowledge of that person); they're more attracted by the status.

If you're seen with a celebrity such as Taylor Swift or Beyoncé, you're immediately much cooler, luckier, and more blessed than your friends and family. However, because people see how celebrities benefit from their degree of status, people want to emulate their social success and seek out symbols of status to garner unconditional acceptance and adoration from their peers. When I first started making online courses, my motives were completely selfish. All I wanted was to become a famous life-coaching teacher; I wanted students and professionals alike to see me as a significant figure in the industry. People think they can prove their significance by buying big houses, going on elaborate holidays, eating expensive foods, and buying designer clothing because capitalism has made them believe that material wealth is the most valuable, effective, and powerful symbol of significance. This is why so many people's lives unravel.

THE DANGER OF PROVING YOUR SIGNIFICANCE

I once worked with a CEO of a major organisation, who I'll call Robert for the purpose of this story. Robert had been in the profession since he was sixteen years old and, by his mid-forties, had worked his way to the top. He had committed over half his life to progressing to the top for the sake of his family who, he admitted, he was becoming estranged from. His work demanded he travel all over the world for weeks and sometimes months at a time. Whilst his job meant he had been able to fully support his wife and children, send his children to the best private schools, and pay for their university fees, it came at a huge price: alienation. His children were adults now and, though they loved each other very much, they didn't know each other very well. He'd missed months of their lives at a time, flickering in and out in short bursts of energy. He hadn't been there through their study stresses or met some of their friends or romantic partners growing up. He'd been there as financial support, but there were thousands of occasions where he couldn't be there emotionally. He knew his children had gone through pains and joys he would never know about and wasn't there to witness. What's more, all he was left with at the end of the day was a glass ceiling.

Robert had spent over half of his life climbing a professional ladder in his industry, only to finally reach the top and find himself feeling totally lost. He'd done it; he'd done every-thing he had been striving to do for decades, and this was all there was. It was like he'd been wading his way through an extremely tricky maze for years and years, only to finally reach the centre of it and find there was nothing there he hadn't already had this entire time. Robert felt, as many people do, that if he wasn't making any progress in life, his life was mean-ingless, and there's an air of truth to that. I'll elaborate more on this in chapter seven, but life is meant to be a journey of growth, and growth is, by definition, progressional. There's a reason why those of us who get stuck in what we perceive as dead-end jobs, relationships, or places become depressed and unmotivated. We need to progress in life in order to feel fulfilled. Because very few of us know how to determine our own significance outside of external factors such as career, wealth, company, and status, we are all vulnerable to falling into this pit of defeatism and purposelessness. What Robert found out the hard way was what I expressed earlier: significance cannot be proven, nor can it be bought.

What Robert and the guy in the supermarket showed me was that when we're too busy trying to prove our significance to the world, we do so at the cost of meaningful connection, acceptance, and a sense of belonging because we live our lives chasing external approval, titles, and status rather than focussing on sharing our authentic selves with others. We can claim to be significant, but unless we're giving people the value we have to offer, they won't see us as significant. True significance is earned when you give others your most valuable commodity: time.

CHAPTER SEVEN

DON'T INHERIT YOUR PARENTS' PANTRY

SO, WHAT ROLE DO CORE VALUES PLAY IN THIS DISCUS-sion and exactly where do they fit in? Core values can be used to help you understand what you actually want in life, which, in turn, helps you prioritise your time and goals. Prioritising your time efficiently helps you achieve inner peace because it encourages you to spend your time on more significant matters rather than time-consuming and emotionally drain-ing activities. If you don't understand or recognise your core values, you'll find yourself drowning in an unending sense of confusion and chaos.

Speaking from personal experience, my values have guided me and helped shape my priorities and reactions in life; they serve as the marker I follow to ensure my life is heading in the direction which is best for me and those around me. They're also pretty handy with letting me know when I've taken a wrong turn in life. I'm sure you know that feeling: that sinking sensation you get when you've done some-thing that doesn't sit well with you, even if it is morally right. Perhaps you've said yes to something you wish you hadn't, invested time and energy into people you weren't sure about, or followed a career and lifestyle you thought you wanted because your parents wanted it for you and found out the hard way that it wasn't for you. Your core values are like your invisible Jiminy Crickets: they're quiet most of the time, so you're never really aware of them until you're going astray—then they show themselves. When your actions and words align with your core values, life is generally pretty great; you feel content, confident, and satisfied. When you're misaligned with your core values and engage in ways which conflict with them, you begin to feel uneasy and wrong. *So it's simple*, I hear you say, *all I need to do is cut out all the core values which make me feel uneasy and abide by the ones which make me feel great*. I'm afraid, my friend, it's not as clear-cut as that.

The problem is, core values are hardly infallible; also, they aren't the same thing as your moral compass. Whilst you would like to think that morality exists as an objective standard, morality, like your core values, is subjective (albeit less obviously so). This is because morals are influenced and determined by your core values. You would like to think that everyone regards certain things in life as immoral, such as murder, cruelty, violence, abuse, and prejudice, but the truth of the matter is that everyone defines the limitations and exemptions to these immoralities differently.

Some people believe all violence is wrong, whereas others believe some violence is wrong, but violence against animals for food is OK. There are those who believe violence in self-defence is acceptable, but to add complexity to the matter, everyone has different ideas of what defines self-defence:

some people would only throw a punch if someone threw one at them, whereas others would throw a punch to defend their honour if someone insulted them verbally. Your core values determine what you deem is morally right, but unfortunately, your core values aren't always inclined to be moral. For example, if one of your core values is wealth, you'll likely feel somewhat comfortable accumulating money deceptively. That doesn't mean you necessarily rob people of money, but you may purposely give the wrong change to a cashier to save yourself fifty pence, or you may not be self-conscious about being a hardcore salesperson who guilts people into parting with their hard-earned money because it's just a job and, according to your philosophy, everyone has to make money somehow.

Core values are the product of your upbringing, environment, culture, status, and experiences. You adopt core values to match (or counteract) your environments and circumstances, which means sometimes your negative life experiences breed negative core values. Of course, you're unaware that they're negative. To you, all of your core values are valid and justified. For example, if you grew up in an unhealthy environment which taught you that life is a constant struggle, you will likely value martyrdom. The funny thing about martyrdom is that those who have it do not see it in themselves, and even fewer recognise martyrdom as one of their core values. However, if you're someone who feels uncomfortable and wrong in moments when you stop feeling depressed or when you're doing well for yourself in life, you, on an unconscious level, value martyrdom. If your suffering, past or present, forms part of your identity, you value martyrdom because it gives your life meaning and definition, whether you're comfortable with that or not.

THE FOUR STAGES OF DEVELOPMENT

As you can see, core values are complex; even shared values between people exist on a spectrum of significance and meaning. People define certain core values differently, even the most general values such as honesty and trust. So, how *exactly* do you develop core values? According to a theory proposed by marketing professor, sociologist, and author of *The People Puzzle*, Morris Massey, values are developed in four stages. Each stage of the theory lays out the generational experiences that produce qualitative differences in attitudes, values, and behaviours in people during different stages of their lives. Whilst generalisations are problematic in many ways (primarily because they overlook significant sociocultural, race, and religious differences), the stages presented in his theory identify relatively universal and easily identifiable broad trends within certain age groups. According to Massey, the four stages of development are:

1. The Imprint Period (age 0 to 7)
2. The Modelling Period (age 8 to 13)
3. The Socialisation Period (age 13 to 21)
4. The Actualisation Period (age 21 to Death)

During the imprint period, people absorb everything, and everything that's absorbed is accepted as truth. Because of children's unquestioning acceptance of the world around them, this period marks the moment when people are most likely to develop early developmental trauma, neurological problems, and the negative core beliefs which come with them. The horrors, no matter how minor or major, stick with people, and because children lack any other form of reference point during this period (such as self-accumulated life experience), they evaluate all positive and negative circumstances in relation to themselves. For example, if your mother was always angry and aggressive, you would naturally internalise her anger and engage in behaviours such as self-blame, self-hatred, and shame; or if your father was always missing and having fights with your other parent, you would naturally feel inclined to believe they were fighting about you.

Nearly all of your behaviours and mannerisms developed in response to those closest to you as part of your fundamental survival technique. Children only have one source of comfort, warmth, and food (i.e., their guardian), so they need to behave in a way which ensures they keep their access to vital resources secure. Children, therefore, are hyper-aware of the emotions they elicit from their primary caregivers and respond in the way most beneficial to them. For example, if their parent is easily angered or critical, a child may develop codependent coping mechanisms to ensure peace; however, if a parent is overly affectionate, a child may lean into this and become more dependent and needy. During the imprinting stage, children are most susceptible to learning what is right and wrong, and they tend to believe that everything their parents do is right, meaning bad behaviours, coping mechanisms, and attitudes are impressed on them. They don't question their parents' mistreatment of them or their loneliness; they regard spending excessive amounts of money as normal; they learn that showing emotions is a sign of weakness, or they believe yelling, cursing, and hitting are justified ways to react when angry.

This leads us neatly onto the modelling period where, as the name suggests, children model the people around them (and the people they admire). They stop blindly accepting everything and begin to seek out and recognise role models. You likely recall teachers, friends, authors, actors, and celebrities who influenced you during this stage in your life, from the hobbies you took up to the fashion fails and bad hairstyles you adopted. There will have been people you tried to be like in every way, from behaviour to looks, slang, interests, and accent. The modelling period extends slightly into the next, but the focus shifts more onto socialisation after the age of thirteen (as evidenced by how influenced teenagers are by their peers). You, like everyone else between the ages of thirteen and twenty-one, just wanted to be accepted and fit in somewhere. During this phase of your life, you may have taken up a career, internship, or degree, or joined a club, religion, organisation, or society to find like-minded people and break away from the models and mindsets you'd been exposed to in early childhood.

The final stage, which you're probably in now, is the journeying stage. This is where you grow out of rules and ignorant beliefs you've picked up naively along the way in the hopes that they'd teach you the correct way to live. Life isn't such an easy manual. Rules, beliefs, and thoughts can be helpful for short, even fleeting, periods of time, but it's not until your actualisation period that you come to recognise the significance and importance of letting things go. People hold on to everything they learn because they believe everything is infinitely useful and beneficial to them when, in reality, most (if not all) things they pick up have either an expiration date or need to be adjusted and reconfigured.

DECLUTTERING YOUR MIND'S PANTRY

Your value system is a bit like a pantry: there are some products which can stay at the back of a shelf for years and years without needing replenishment, but there are other goods you get through quicker or that you may want to update and switch around to spice life up a little. You may have some goods in there which have been there for so long that you haven't checked the expiration date in years and they need throwing out, whilst there are other things you just keep adding in for the sake of it, like fancy flax seeds, chia seeds, and raspberry vinaigrette, which you know you will never use but you bought anyway because it was trendy at the time, and everyone was talking about them on social media.

Grounded and well-organised adults clear out their mind pantries on a regular basis. They have the self-awareness to know and accept that not everything in there is going to last forever. Things need replenishing, updating, and discarding accordingly, and the more familiar they are with the contents and usefulness of their mind pantry, the more at rest and productive they are with their lives. They know there is no right way to live, and they know they shouldn't just inherit and mimic the pantry their parents left them with—it's stale, old, and inauthentic to who they are. People who keep their parents' old pantry are those who never challenge the system they were born into. They prioritise conforming and fitting into the society and culture around them because they were taught to be suspicious of individuality and uniqueness at the cost of their own authenticity.

Actualisation involves the unlearning of and unsubscribing from the unhelpful and negative beliefs you have entrenched in your psyche by engaging with the tools of curiosity. By forcing yourself to reflect on your beliefs and on what you know, you develop a deeper insight into the layers you've unconsciously built up around your sense of self. It's only through asking the difficult questions and challenging your beliefs and values that you begin to uncover the unhelpful factors which have been holding you back in life and develop a new perspective on how you came to be the way you are.

I know what you're thinking: that's all very well and good, talking about the significance of core values, but how on earth are you supposed to identify them? Well, I'm sure you value trust, loyalty, peace, generosity, honesty, growth, empathy, truthfulness, efficiency, and things similar to those. Most people do. Identifying things you value is technically easy, but having too many values to abide by can be overwhelming and mentally exhausting. Therefore, it's important to limit your number of core values and strive to fulfil a selection of them to the best of your capabilities.

The first step to uncovering what you truly value in life is to get real with yourself and stop viewing yourself through rose-tinted glasses. When it comes to personal self-evaluation, even the most insecure and self-deprecating person prefers to view themselves in an overly idealistic way. Most people regard themselves as kinder, friendlier, more generous, and more supportive than they really are. This means that most people tend to claim values they know they *should* have rather than those they actually do.

DEFINING YOUR CORE VALUES

You can't pick your values. You can only discover them through your actions and thoughts. Judging your legitimate and upheld values takes a lot of honesty, acceptance, and tough love, but it's more than possible provided you take the time to sit down and reflect. The most effective approach to uncovering your core values is to write down all the significant moments in life, good and bad, which taught you something, because these experiences will reflect the values you either acquire or oppose. You may have witnessed something you agreed or disagreed with, accomplished something which fulfilled you, or been through something which evoked an unexpected response from you. Only you know what the most significant moments of your life are, and only you can dissect them to identify what values are hidden within those moments.

Once you have a list of values, it's time to narrow them down, but this is obviously difficult for many. After all, most values are (arguably) important to some degree, so choosing to discard and dismiss them in favour of others can feel daunting. You could write down hundreds of core values you'd ideally like to hold yourself accountable to, but you know in your heart of hearts that such a list is unrealistic. If you've ever decluttered your home, you will know that organising anything in life usually requires that you make a horrendous mess first before you can put things into place, so start by word-vomiting all the values you truly uphold before categorising them. If you have lots of related or very similar values, find one word which best describes them all, then cull the ones which aren't as important as others. The best approach to weeding out casual values from core ones is to ask yourself which values represent who you truly are and support who you want to grow into. Those are the only ones which truly matter. The rest are just accessories to your sense of being.

Challenge yourself to list between five and ten core values. These core values are the ones you will subsequently carry through your life and demonstrate through daily actions, so it's important you formulate a list which supports both your strengths and weaknesses. Of course, the process is one of trial and error, so give yourself the time to learn, adjust, and amend when necessary. I would recommend that you start off with a list of ten core values and then challenge yourself to implement and act upon them for thirty days. By the end of thirty days, return to your list and evaluate your progress and values. Ask yourself which ones came naturally, which ones felt misplaced, and which ones were too difficult. Were there values you excluded from your list which you missed and would like to implement onto your list, or were there values which didn't feel right and you'd like to remove and replace?

Over the next few weeks, keep working on your core values by taking the time to consciously act in accordance with them, and spend time evaluating how you feel at the end of the day or week. It's important that you make decisions in accordance with your true values, so any feelings of misalignment, inauthenticity, or emptiness need to be addressed through the evaluation of your core values. I would recommend working on a list of values for at least a month before making any major changes to your list (unless you recognise very early on in your self-examination that one of your values is grossly inappropriate for who you're trying to become). Once you've formulated a successful list of values, cement it and carry it consciously throughout every priority decision you face in life.

CHAPTER EIGHT

THE VALUE OF A PRODUCTIVE LIFE

LET'S ELABORATE ON THE TOPIC WE TOUCHED ON IN the last chapter: progress. Progression is a universal core value; whether it's for professional or personal reasons, everyone wants to be productive and progress forward in life. I've never heard anyone say 'I hope my life, myself, and the world around me stays exactly how it is now forever and ever, unchanged for all eternity'. You may have said something similar in romantic or joyous moments of passion or excitement with loved ones, friends, and family, but they're not sincere wishes. Nobody wants to freeze their life in a moment forever; even the most fun moments will become boring after a while (which is why we don't have Christmas every day, kids).

The kind of progression I will discuss in this chapter is one which revolves around the challenges, obstacles, and hardships you're expected to overcome to move forward and develop a better state of being. There are a lot of things you probably wish to see progress in life: yourself, your friends and family, society, politics, cultural acceptance, and environmental consciousness, but if you were truly honest with yourself, you'd have to admit you aren't doing much to help these things progress. Most people with low self-confidence tend to feel a degree of shame and inferiority about their perceived inability to get things done or execute tasks to the standard they'd hoped they would. Their dependence on external validation means they tread so lightly that they end up trapped in a comfort zone. Speaking from a practical standpoint, staying in one's comfort zone has a logical justification: it's ideal for keeping the world predictable, safe, and steady. Yet whilst working from one's comfort zone may ensure steady and predictable results, maximum performance can only be achieved with the aid of a little anxiety. Not too much, obviously—paralysis is a serious issue—but when it comes to productivity, the Goldilocks equilibrium of anxiety is the best: not too much anxiety but not too little.

BREAKING OUT OF YOUR COMFORT ZONE

I get it; taking a leap of faith and living a life of unpredictable results can be terrifying, especially when you have low self-confidence. Establishing a healthy work-life balance is hard enough in this fast-paced world. The last thing you probably want to do is add the pressure of juggling additional anxiety and chaos. Why would anyone want to incorporate more fear and anxiety into their existing state of never-ending busyness when it already feels unmanageable? Well, crazily enough, because it will do you good.

Most people think keeping themselves busy means not living in their comfort zone because their idea of a comfort zone is lazing around at home, lying in front of the TV, or slacking off at work. However, the *comfort* in comfort zone is misleading. You can be in your comfort zone and still feel stressed the max, running around with a to-do list the length of an A4 piece of paper, working in a job you hate, and coming home to a relationship you know died out years ago. Comfort zones are not cosy havens of contentment and inactivity—they're hamster wheels you're willingly keeping yourself in out of fear of the unknown.

Living a life you don't enjoy and that wears you down does not indicate you're living a life out of your comfort zone, nor does it mean you're living a productive life. I hate to be the bearer of bad news, but busyness and productivity are not the same thing. It's incredibly fashionable nowadays to post statuses online to your friends and followers complaining about how busy you are and how the hustle is real. However, the reality is that your unsustainable busyness is nothing more than a mask for the fear which drives you unrelentlessly every day.

Routines can be dangerous traps to fall into, but don't get me wrong; I'm not here to discourage having routines in life. Having a routine is a powerful mindfulness exercise: waking up and going to sleep at the same time, eating the same meals, or walking the quickest and most effective way to work helps keep you focused and less disorientated on a daily basis. But breaking those routines is as important for your mental well-being as diet and exercise. The benefits of brain exercises (such as crosswords and mind puzzles) are well known, but very few know how changing one's routines and stepping out of a comfort zone can have an equally beneficial impact on their brain. Performing on autopilot all the time is not only a bad habit for your brain to fall into, but it can be incredibly dangerous. Running your brain on autopilot is just like driving a car on autopilot: it may be safe to accidentally slip into

ate when driving now and then, but you'd be
fe and others' lives at risk if you relied on your
) autopilot mode every time you drove to work.
ient is always changing. Every day you wake up,
with new risks and unexpected factors, so your
brain needs to be sharp enough to adapt effectively.

Challenging your brain doesn't mean you need to overhaul
your routines every few weeks or take up expensive classes and
therapies. Keeping your brain on its toes can be as simple as
changing one thing a day, like taking a different route to work,
prepping or buying a new meal to have that day, exercising at
a different time, or talking to a new person. If you really want
to put your brain to the test, start learning a language for free
online, take up a new hobby like climbing or drawing, crack
open a board game with friends on the weekend, or learn that
musical instrument you always wanted to as a child.

None of these suggestions may sound like risks, but they
technically are for those with low self-confidence. When your
confidence is so low that you're too afraid of failing or being
terrible at something, breaking your rhythm in any way is risky.
You're risking proving yourself wrong, humiliating yourself, or
being bad and failing at something. Despite what your inner
critic keeps telling you, you have the ability to learn new things
and solve new problems. You just need to break this pattern
of thinking in order to do so. Taking smaller risks to challenge
your self-concept is part of the personal growth process. If
you're frightened of making mistakes, don't be. The bigger
the mistakes you make, the bigger the lessons you learn, and
the more confident you'll become in your ability to thrive and
overcome. You will never know how you respond to chaos,
disaster, and mess until you experience them. After that, there

are two options: you can choose to learn and grow from these circumstances, or you can choose to become a victim and wallow in self-pity, putting your life on hold and drowning in insecurity, fears, and victimhood.

THE FORMULA FOR GETTING THE RESULTS YOU WANT

Stagnation in life causes people to wander aimlessly in boring and meaningless circles. When you feel depressingly unfulfilled, you will do everything to keep yourself busy: from working overtime at the job you hate to overworking at the gym or over-socialising. As I stated earlier, keeping busy and being productive are very different things, although they're commonly confused by those emotionally invested in being a busybody. The distinguishing factor between keeping busy and being productive is that productivity demands that you step out of your comfort zone and take risks in the midst of uncertainty. Busyness, on the other hand, relies on you pottering around your comfort zone, usually in an effort to mask procrastination. Very few people are comfortable playing with uncertainty because, as I discussed in chapter five, very few people are willing to invest their energy in faith rather than fear.

Pursuing a bigger and greater life than the one you're currently living will always be a risk, but it's the only way you can break new barriers, discover more about your abilities and limits, become wiser and more informed, and learn more about the world around you. I can't think of a single meaningful thing that happened in my life that wasn't the result of a risk I took—from finances to career choices, relationship decisions, and business ventures. Luckily, there is a formula you can follow in order to achieve anything you want to in life, but I didn't discover it until I went to a children's birthday party a few years ago.

I know, children's birthday parties aren't renowned for being the most suitable places for profound enlightenment. I think even the Dalai Lama would struggle to channel mindful thought in the midst of a screaming, sticky mosh pit of ice-cream-and-cake-fuelled children. Having no children myself, I wasn't someone who spent a lot of time around them a few years ago. To me, they seemed like an alien species who communicated in a whole other language, both physically and verbally, and that somewhat intimidated me. I'd never been to a children's birthday party since having been a child myself, and after years in the army, I was anxious about how I'd come across to a small human who, let's face it, wouldn't have the discipline or self-control I was used to. The last thing I wanted was to be seen as a stuck-up, boring, rigid, serious guy by children. So, a few weeks before the party, I began researching online how to entertain children at a party (i.e., ways to be seen as cool at a children's party). After a few minutes of searching, I found the answer: balloon animals.

Believe it or not, balloon animals are not that hard to make once you've spent a couple of weekends practising, and not just balloon animals but also balloon hats, balloon flowers, balloon swords, even balloon Teenage Mutant Ninja Turtles. I noticed that as the party date came closer and closer, my anxiety about the situation lessened. Needless to say, I was the coolest thing at the party (or so I'd like to believe). It wasn't until I came away from an amazing Saturday surrounded by kids and colourful balloons that I realised the only reason my anxiety and worries subsided was because of a strategy. In order to understand how this strategy formulated itself, let's break down my thought process:

1. I was invited to a children's party, an environment which I wasn't familiar or comfortable with; therefore, I felt anxious.
2. What was I anxious about? I was anxious about coming across as boring and rigid to other people because I was an ex-soldier who wasn't used to being around children.
3. So, I asked myself: what results do I want? Do I want to be the uncool, silent, and scary man at a party who doesn't join in and doesn't try to, or do I want to be a cool, fun, and friendly guy who came prepared to have fun with everyone?
4. Once I determined what outcome I wanted, I then thought of solutions that would produce the outcome I desired.

That thought process can be neatly summarised into the following equation:

Desire + Strategy + Ability = Result

There are three things you need in life in order to overcome your limiting beliefs and make progress: a desire for an outcome, a strategy for how you intend to make that outcome a reality, and the skills or effort necessary to implement that strategy. You can have the desire to become a published author, but unless you've planned a book or written the book, you'll never become a published author. You can be an amazing artist with incredible skills, but unless you have the desire to make artwork your income and have a strategy to market yourself as a professional artist, you'll never become one. The strategy part of the equation will always, without question, involve stepping out of your comfort zone because it's the nature of the equation. If you keep doing what you've always done, you're never going to have more than what you already have. That sounds like common sense when I put it in writing, but I've met a staggering number of people who are genuinely shocked, depressed, and confused that they're not getting the results they want, despite never changing anything about their life and how they go about accomplishing things.

A lot of people are far too comfortable waiting for life to happen to them rather than making life happen for them. They think that if they sit on their computer long enough, someone will randomly hit them up on LinkedIn and give them the opportunity of a lifetime, or their boss will just approach them one day and give them a raise. Having everything fall into your lap just at the right time is how progression works in films and books, but not in reality. There aren't successful Samaritans lurking in the corners of your future, just waiting for their time to pop up into your life and give you all the opportunities, success, and standing you've ever asked for. The only way you can make any progress in life is to start making the ways for yourself and accepting the blowbacks and hits you get along the way.

FULFILMENT VERSUS HAPPINESS

Progress starts with a vision; you won't progress in life without having a vision for your future and ideal outcomes. Desired outcomes in life should be those that are fundamentally fulfilling in nature rather than gratifying. Gratification, like happiness, is a short-lived experience. A good meal can be gratifying, receiving an award can be gratifying, even winning money is gratifying, but that buzz you get the moment it happens will always extinguish. It may take a few minutes, a few hours, or even a few days, but the buzz of happiness and gratification always dies out, which is why you're so addicted to chasing it. You eat more food, drink more, spend more money, take more photos, and post more on social media because the buzz of happiness they bring isn't capable of sustaining you for long.

Fulfilment, on the other hand, isn't related to or affected by your emotions; you can go through tragedy but still feel fulfilled in life. Fulfilment is not as slippery or prone to distortion as happiness is. Instead, fulfilment exists as a form of mental nourishment, whereas happiness is like a sugary doughnut or energy drink, which you immediately feel the effects of. Happiness gives you an adrenaline rush, but once you're on that high you only have two choices: you either allow yourself to crash and burn or you continue chasing the sugar-laden frenzy by consuming more. On the other hand, fulfilment acts like protein; you don't feel the energy it gives you because it's more subtle than that of sugar, nor do you realise it's keeping your cravings at bay, but it keeps you content and satisfied enough to carry on and focus on what you want to do.

Unlike happiness, achieving fulfilment isn't always easy and pleasant. It requires a degree of effort. Fulfilment demands that you evaluate your options, make wiser decisions, learn more about yourself, and understand why you do the things you do. In order to progress in life, you need to fully understand how and why you tick (i.e., what values are driving you) so that you can pursue what you want out of life rather than what you *think* you want. This is where most people get lost. Very few people know where they want to go in life because they're indecisive; they're either overwhelmed with the choice or underwhelmed by themselves and their capabilities. Such indecisiveness always results in people either opting to do nothing or opting to do everything; neither option proves a successful equation for productivity.

PRODUCTIVITY DEMANDS YOU DO LESS

Life is constructed of trade-offs: everything you do in life comes at the cost of everything you don't. You can't put 100 percent meaningful effort, energy, or passion into everything you'd like to in life; progress and mastery require exclusion. You can't be an Olympic athlete or a famous singer and actor who stars in Hollywood films who studied medicine and has a family who they spend all their free time with whilst also finding the time to write a bestseller, go to the gym three times a week, and travel the world on a regular basis. Granted, you can do all of these things on some level throughout your lifetime. You can play sports, go to the gym, write a book, travel the world, act in a play, and sing, but you can't achieve all of them to the greatest standard you want all at the same time.

You can't do everything at once. In order to make progress in life, you need to microfocus in on one thing and dedicate your life to it for an extensive period of time. The same goes for values: if you value security in life, you do so at the cost of freedom; if you value certainty, you do so at the cost of valuing risk, and if you value independence, you do so at the risk of valuing connection. If you want to live a productive life with a strong sense of self-awareness, you need to identify and understand the parameters of your core values. You need to understand that your values exist on an unconscious scale of significance and that this scale is pivotal in assessing where your energy is best spent.

Unless you define and refine your values on a regular basis, you'll never have the clarity you need to motivate yourself out of bed every morning. Without defined values, you'll find your life will always lack a degree of clarity and direction. If you don't understand or consider the values underpinning your motivations in life, you will never be able to efficiently prioritise your objectives, routines, projects, or relationships when you think of your life in terms of the big picture, that is, the overarching story that is your life. In terms of the big picture, are you honestly mainly driven by your desire for a nice new car, home, or annual holiday? Whilst these things may motivate you in the short term, they're not likely to be your motivation for living a long, healthy, fulfilled life.

Because you, like the rest of humanity, are merely a cog in a corporate machine, you believe it's normal and valuable to commit your life to earning a living and paying your bills, even if you do so through a job you hate. According to the philosophy you've subconsciously subscribed to, the money you earn is more important than your enjoyment of the job. You rarely take the time to ask yourself why you do the things you do because, on an unconscious level, you don't think there should be another reason other than earning money and building your sense of significance.

I don't have a career as a balloon-animal maker; I'm not a children's party entertainer, and I don't teach balloon-animal making. On the surface level, most people would consider my time learning how to make balloon animals a waste. It didn't go towards making me any money or towards evolving my employable skillset. It was useful for a day, but that was it. People wouldn't consider my balloon-animal-making skills progressive in any shape or form, but that's because people have a skewed idea of what progress really means. They see progress as climbing up the corporate ladder, getting promotions, earning more money, building a family, getting married, or becoming better at a skill. These things can symbolise progress in life, but only if they change you for the better.

Progress isn't just about making improvements in your life; it's about offering the world around you your most valuable self as you grow and develop as an individual. Anyone can get a promotion at a job, but not everyone can be a meaningful boss or colleague who helps bring others up with them. Anyone can make a family, but not everyone can raise conscientious children who appreciate what they have in life and are driven by a desire to make the world a better place. Anyone can become an artist, but not every artist strives to make a meaningful impact with their work which improves the socio-political climate in their local neighbourhood and spends their time helping get underprivileged children and people into the arts. As I stated in the previous chapter, your significance in life cannot be self-directed or dictated; it's only determined by others based on the value you give them. The question is: what exactly is your value and how can you give it?

CHAPTER NINE

HOW VALUABLE ARE YOU?

WHILST I'VE MENTIONED MY ARMY BACKGROUND OVER the last few chapters, I haven't really gone in depth about it, so let's talk about it here. I never felt valued as an individual growing up. I came from that stereotypical, traditional upbringing where children should be seen and not heard, a phrase which I'm grateful is dying out—it's a patronising and dangerous lesson to teach children. Sure, they can be noisy, which is irritating to even the most patient of adults, but enforcing this idea that a child should be seen and not heard teaches a child that their opinions, voice, and thoughts aren't valid. Children can't distinguish between the lessons that apply to them in youth and the lessons which apply to them in adulthood. You teach them to be a particular way in childhood, and they're most likely going to remain that way in adulthood. Therefore, if you teach them to be quiet and keep their opinions to themselves when they're young, they're not going to know when that rule stops applying to them. Can they start speaking at six, ten, thirteen, or eighteen years old? When do they stop only being seen and not heard?

This ridiculous philosophy was applied to me and it, of course, made little, rebellious me a noisy, cheeky child. However, no matter how loud and cheeky I was, I never got the kind of attention I craved. I was never taken seriously or listened to, and I was always being told off, regardless of whether the scolding was warranted or not. It probably didn't help that I wasn't a child who excelled in obvious areas like school or sports. I had no passion for any of the subjects I was taught, and I wasn't the athletic type (football was never my thing). Because I didn't have that natural flair that other kids seemed to have, my parents and teachers gave up on me quite early. Why encourage someone to try who obviously isn't naturally capable? Children pick up the attitudes of their guardians; if their teachers and parents regard them as a failure, then they'll see themselves like that too. For me, it made me feel totally worthless in life. What could I possibly have to offer that was of any value to anyone? Me, with my scrawny chicken legs and bad grades. I wasn't ticking any of society's boxes, and in the eyes of my parents and school, it seemed that I was just growing up into a waste of space and, let me tell you, they made me feel it. I felt like a waste of space; which is why, at age sixteen, I decided to join the army.

I wanted to do something significant with my life to compensate for the lack of significance I felt in myself: not just significant, irrefutably significant. The army, therefore, was perfect. No one could deny my significance. I won the approval of my peers, friends, family, and women (especially with the help of a few fabricated stories about my time in war zones). However, when I finally left the military, having become bored with the rules and conformity, I was a drunken, amoral mess. In fact, the biggest mistake I made in life was how badly I handled the transition from military to civilian life. Though, really, with the lack of help out there for ex-service people, what could anyone really expect? From the age of sixteen, my life had been nothing but the army for nearly nine years. I lived, breathed, and thought like a soldier; my entire identity was wound up in the uniform I wore. Then one day, with the click of my fingers, I was back in the same world I'd left when I was a child. Here I was, back at home in my hometown with my parents. I had no job, no home of my own, no ranking, no girlfriend, and was of no value to anyone. It was like nothing had happened. The army had just been a hazy daydream and all I was left with were unaddressed and suppressed symptoms of PTSD, depression, and anxiety my military service had given me. I didn't know how to work through my experiences or feelings, so I turned to drugs, crime, and alcohol.

Within a few short years, I ruined my credibility and reputation and ruined my life and the lives around me. I've been arrested for being drunk and disorderly, and for causing grievous bodily harm, I've spent nights in police cells, done months of community service, lost my driver's licence, and been fined hundreds of pounds. I've been caught driving under the influence twice, and I even once assaulted an innocent man because I was in such a dark place of self-hatred and frustration. I used to use women all the time and treated their emotions unkindly because I only wanted pleasure from them and saw them as nothing more than that.

You're probably wondering why on earth anyone would share their dirty laundry in a book which can be read by hundreds, potentially thousands of people. Am I proud of any of this? I'll never be proud; I spent many years of my life in shame and regret over everything I'd done. I have no excuses for my behaviour other than my inability to control and manage my emotions. However, whilst I'm not proud of my scandalous past, I'm not ashamed of it, either, because I have the confidence in who I am today to know I am not that man anymore. People may judge me based on my past, but I know how far I've come and how much I've evolved and transformed from who I was. I'm not so proud as to deny my wrongdoings in life; I've taken ownership and responsibility for everything I did and everything I learned from those mistakes. There is no circumstance or person to blame for what I went through other than myself. I'm an autonomous being with my own thoughts and actions, and no amount of depression, childhood trauma, anxiety, and PTSD can excuse away what I did.

My past is part of who I am today, and I wouldn't be who I am today without having gone through what I did. Everyone has skeletons in their closet, but self-shame, be it for their past or present self, is destructive and unhelpful to carry. I know your past is not squeaky clean, and I know you've done and said things you shouldn't have. You're in no position to judge me, because there's someone out there with even cleaner hands than you who can judge you in return. Only I know my true intentions in life, as only you do yours, so whilst there may be strangers who will pass judgment on you and your past, accusing you of being malicious for things that you've done, only you know the validity of that sentiment and, therefore, you don't need to give other people's opinions any more thought than that. It's easy to take people's judgments to heart; you may go out of your way to prove others wrong, but some minds can't be changed. The only mind you need to focus on changing is yours—you need to change your opinion of yourself and no one else's. As long as you can prove yourself wrong and become proud of who you evolve into, no one else's opinions matter.

EMBRACE YOUR MISTAKES

Shame that is toxic to the point of paralysis is very different from guilt, which can be a healthy motivator for you to make positive changes in your life. Shame leads to self-deprecating language and feelings of worthlessness, because it focuses on the idea that you *are* something bad rather than you've done something bad. Your actions do not define you; in the same way, your job, family, looks, or accent doesn't define you. Most people regularly fall into the trap of defining their value by these external factors; you likely believe that every failure you have depletes your value, that your salary equates your value, and that your body shape defines your social value. People all fall into this trap because they've been indoctrinated into a system which treats them like commodities: they sell their time to pay the rent and survive; they wear advertisements for companies, and they sell even more of their time to fund social media platforms and streaming services.

People are used to being seen and treated as nothing more than currency. You live in a world where certain people who look and act a certain way are of more value to the system than others, and yet you wonder why your head is so messed up. You've become so crushed by the system, your past, and your failures that you have overlooked your worth and what you have to offer the world (which, trust me, you have an abundance of), and instead you have focused on your commodifiable value.

You have made mistakes in life: some catastrophic, others just unpleasant or embarrassing. Whatever your mistakes are, regret is a waste of emotional energy to feel towards them. Every mistake you make is a learning opportunity, no matter how severe it is. I've made small fortunes off businesses and lost every penny and ended up losing homes. I've fallen in love and then made a fool of myself and lost those dearest to me. These embarrassing, shameful, and painful emotions like to rear their ugly heads when you're in a dark mental place, but that doesn't mean they have to destroy your day, week, or life.

You can't suppress, forget, and ignore those memories, nor can you stop them from spontaneously resurfacing when your guard is down. The only thing you can do is change how you feel about them. The next time that embarrassing or horrifying memory enters your mind, rather than cringing at how awful a person you were and how you deserve all the bad things that ever happened to you, be thankful that you've learned to never do, say, think, or act in that way ever again (well, to not be that way consciously, because we all make mistakes, and change takes time).

OWN YOUR STORY

The key to managing your emotions and self-critical thoughts when bad memories arise is disassociating your past self from your present. You are not the person you were ten years ago, and you don't have to be the person you were yesterday, provided you're willing to take responsibility for and ownership of what your past self did, mistakes and all. Growth, maturity, and being a better person requires conscious effort; you can't just expect these things to come naturally with age; they're not a right of passage. You have to choose whether or not you want to learn, grow, and develop from your past.

Your value doesn't lie in the mistakes or achievements you make in life; it lies in the lessons you take away from them. You can't share mistakes and achievements with others, but you can share lessons. I share my failures with people because I want to help others who have gone through what I've gone through recognise that they are capable of completely transforming their life. I want people to realise that they're not inherently inferior, that they aren't destined to be a bum and a loser, that their failures are not predetermined or destined to repeat themselves.

It's easy to look at your past and determine what went wrong—who you lost, what happened to you, why you lost opportunities, or what other people did to you—and conclude that all the bad things which happened to you were deserved or predestined according to your genetics. However, nothing you've gone through was deserved, fated, or plotted against you. This is just your story. Your story is what makes you unique and valuable to other people and the world around you. Society wouldn't be where it is today if people stopped sharing their stories with one another. Every significant positive change in society comes from someone overcoming something in life and deciding that this story is worth acting upon, this story needs sharing, this story needs awareness, and this story needs to bring change in the world so others going through the same story don't have to feel alone and unsupported.

From social movements to educational, cultural, and scientific developments, every important movement started with a story. Your past is what gives you meaning today, from every rejection, failure, heartbreak, and pain you went through. Your past is what has given you the strength, determination, skills, values, insight, wisdom, and nurture necessary for you to be here today, reading this book.

You have probably spent most of your life evaluating your

worthiness according to daily outcomes. If you're a parent, you likely determine how good or bad you are based on your child's emotional response; they have a tantrum because you didn't buy them that toy, and you immediately feel like a bad parent. If you're a student, you will evaluate how good a student you are based on how long and hard you study and what grades you produce, or you may value yourself according to your salary and how much work you did on a particular day. Whilst all of these scenarios are different, they follow the same equation for self-evaluation:

What I do + How well I do it = Who I am

In my case, I was a soldier for eight years, and a darn good one at that. Once I ceased being a soldier, the equation fell apart. I had no identity and, thus, no value. We'll talk about finding one's identity more in the following chapters, but for now, we're just going to isolate this equation in terms of determining one's value. Naturally, this equation works absolute wonders when it comes to failures and the cementing of one's value as worthless. If you are a student, but you're not a good student, you're a failure; if you're an entrepreneur, but you've gone bankrupt in your first year in business, you're a failed entrepreneur; if you're a mother who always feels as though she's getting it wrong, you're a bad mother.

This equation, as you can see, is fundamentally flawed; its very foundations are unstable because each part of it is susceptible to flux. According to daily circumstances, the equation needs amending and adjusting, resulting in an inconstant calculation of self which, in turn, utterly destroys people's mental well-being. Yet, despite the stress and chaos this method brings to your life, you stick with it, because after a lifetime of determining your value according to your outcomes, it's difficult to understand that there's a possible alternative evaluation process.

THE EQUATION YOU SHOULD LIVE YOUR LIFE BY

So, let's create a totally unrealistic and impossible scenario. Imagine yourself floating in space in total darkness; you're alive, but you can't see or hear anything, not even your own body. All you can see around you is total darkness, but you still have all your own thoughts and feelings. Are you worthless? Those of you with low self-esteem will probably reply yes, you are literally a waste of space in this form. In that case, change the scenario. Think of the person you love the most and imagine them being the person floating in total darkness, unable to see or hear anything around them; it may be your child, your mother, your partner, your pet, or your best friend. Do you consider them a totally worthless waste of space in this circumstance? Even if this scenario were real, part of you wouldn't be able to draw that harsh conclusion because you love them so much, they're still worth something to you, and when you think of them in this dark space, you wish you could reach out to them and tell them how much they mean to you, how special they are, how much you love them.

This impossible, unrealistic scenario is very much like death: when you lose a loved one, you don't regard them as worthless and meaningless just because they can't see or hear you anymore. In death, they don't have a job, they aren't showing off their talents, they aren't bringing in the money or working incredibly hard day in and out, yet they are still valuable to you. They still have an intrinsic value that's left behind, which had nothing to do with their body, weight, career, wealth, appearance, or possessions. You have this intrinsic value as well, but your low self-esteem prevents you from acknowledging it.

The value you have by just breathing air and being in the world is your true value, and people around can see it. That stranger who smiled at you in the supermarket or your colleague who always talks to you at lunchtime can see and feel your intrinsic value; they know you're not worthless, and they recognise that you're capable of becoming even more valuable if you try to be. If I didn't actively commit myself to be a loving, dependable, open, giving, and honest person, no one would see me as such. How you choose to be today and tomorrow determines how people will see you. If you don't demonstrate your loving nature to someone, they're not going to consider you a loving person, no matter how much you think you are or stress yourself as such.

People don't remember what you bought them for Christmas five years ago, how hard you worked at your job last month, or how famous you became on Instagram. They remember the negative and positive impact you made on them. In other words, people don't remember what you did as much as how you made them *feel*. People remember you not for your career, what you bought them, or your successes and failures, but for who you are: that person whose personality, energy, thoughts, and vibe made them feel a certain way about themselves and about the time they spent with you.

This means that less effort and energy should be put into your talents, skills, careers, and appearance, and more should be put into being your authentic self. This isn't to say your careers, talents, and skills aren't important aspects of your life, but most people put a disproportionate amount of energy into these fields of life at the cost of working on being authentic. People stop working on themselves. They stop paying attention to how they treat others; how they manage their thoughts, moods, and emotions; how they spend their time with others; and where they invest their energy. Instead, they become focused on investing time and growth into superficial markers of value and significance. People assume that leaving a legacy requires that they build, create, or establish something which has a cultural impact on society, but legacies don't have to be that grand a gesture. The personal legacy you leave is just as fruitful and meaningful as any cultural legacy—the legacy of who you were and the lives you touched is just as important, and it doesn't demand you spend money, start a company, or write a book.

Allowing yourself to be who you are, flaws and all, full of past and future mistakes but having an open mind is enough. People will do better in some areas than you in life, and people will try to overtake you and put you down, but nobody can ever be the expert of your life other than you. You are the greatest expert of your experiences, feelings, values, and thoughts. Nobody has access to the concoction of your mind and, therefore, nobody can reach your potential other than you. Your value lies in the fact that you've overcome things in your history, be they small or large, which people can learn from. You have thrived and you have fallen, but the fact that you're reading this book proves that you've climbed back up again, no matter how painful and difficult it was. You have insights and lessons that are unique to you and, therefore, valuable to everyone, even those who have gone through similar experiences.

So, let's take a look at our original yet corrupted equation for self-evaluation one last time:

What I do + How well I do it = Who I am

Take note of it and screw it. The next time you're in a dark, self-critical place, ask yourself if you're trying to align yourself to fit within this equation. You're not the result of your actions. You exist before your actions do; therefore, who you are cannot be a result. The correct equation you need to ensure you follow in life when assessing your value is this:

Who I am + How I am = What I do

In other words, who you are and your nature determine what you should be doing in life. You shouldn't be driven in life by what you do, but instead by who you are and what you value. Sure, we can't all pick ideal careers or live in certain places because life isn't as clear-cut as that, but it doesn't mean we stop striving for a better fit. Who you are should come first and foremost in life, then how you are (and how you demonstrate you are what you are) comes second, whether you're loving, generous, kind, thankful, positive, caring, honest, passionate, calming, or supportive. Take note of how you demonstrate and live up to aspects of your character, good and bad, and amend as you see fit. How can you demonstrate certain parts of your nature more, what parts of your nature are you suppressing, and what parts of your nature would you like to manage better?

'But wait', I hear you ask. 'I know how I am (for the most part), but how am I supposed to live by this equation if I still don't know *who* I am?' My friend, you're not the only one who asks that, so let's talk about it.

CHAPTER TEN

YOU'RE NOT A PRODUCT: YOU SHOULDN'T COME WITH A LABEL

ONE DAY, AS HE SAT BESIDE A LAKE IN GLORIOUS AUS-tralia, a crow minding his own business heard a small voice call up to him. 'Hello, Mr Crow', the voice cried. 'May I ask for some help?'

The crow, curious, looked down to his side and leapt in horror at the sight of a tarantula, a beast which, he knew, had a reputation for biting crows.

'Don't be alarmed!' the tarantula insisted. 'I promise, I'm not here to bite you! I just need some help. My family lives across the other side of the lake, but I've hurt my leg, and I'm afraid to leave them alone for so long without me. Would you please fly me across the lake? I promise, I'll cling to your back but I won't hurt you.'

The crow had heard all about the terrible things tarantulas

...ad done to his kind and refused to help. 'I'm sorry', the crow replied. 'But I don't trust your kind. You've killed many crows I've known, and I can't take the risk.'

'Oh please, I swear on my life that I won't hurt you', the tarantula pleaded. 'My children are all alone and I would hate to make them worry any longer. Please, don't judge my whole kind by the few you've heard of; we're not all like that. I'm not those tarantulas; I'm an individual. Besides, it would be stupid of me to bite you when you're carrying me across a lake. If you go down, I would go down with you and drown!'

The crow was dubious and scared, but the tarantula seemed so sincere that he eventually submitted himself and agreed to fly the tarantula over the lake. He lowered his neck and allowed the tarantula to climb onto his back. True to his word, the tarantula climbed up without biting him and held on to the crow's neck feathers with his little legs. The flight across the lake went smoothly and in silence; the crow even sometimes forgot the tarantula was on his back until he felt the sudden tightening of a tiny grip on his neck feathers. He was almost across the lake when, suddenly, he felt a sharp pinch in his neck. The tarantula had bitten him.

'You horrible, nasty beast', the crow screamed. 'You lied to me! You promised, and now we're both going to die!'

'I couldn't help it', the tarantula replied. 'I'm a tarantula; it's in my nature.'

With that, the crow and tarantula fell into the lake and drowned.

Reading that fable should make you feel angry, not only for

the crow but also for the mes_____ ends. _____
that judgment is warranted_____ople to_____
against a group of people b_____ __ ___ actions, beliefs, an_
behaviours of a select few. Most people vehemently disagree
with this practice; they believe that those who paint groups of
people with the same brush breed hatred and violence with
their ignorance and closed-mindedness. However, many
people uphold prejudices subconsciously, even those who
consider themselves liberally minded. You most likely have
certain places, people, movements, groups, and even shops
and styles of clothing predefined in your mind, and you believe
your prejudices are valid due to certain personal experiences
or things you've read on the internet. Even in your accepting
and open mind, there will be certain tarantulas who you will
always uphold a stereotyped, prejudged perception of regardless of whether they prove themselves otherwise.

THE DANGER OF BOXING YOURSELF IN

Labels are powerful weapons people use against others in
order to establish a hierarchical ranking system within cul-
tures and societies. People are labelled by the things they do,
the music they listen to, the types of clothes they wear, the
religion they follow, their sexuality, their familial status, their
class, and their economic standing. Whilst the tarantula fable
may have a dangerous and negative message you don't agree
with, there is undoubtedly someone (or something) you are
prejudiced against; and if it's not someone else, it's yourself.

People with low self-esteem are hypercritical of both themselves and others to a dangerous fault. You may have lied when
you were thirteen and still refer to yourself as a liar in your thirties, or you may have cheated in your twenties and still think

of yourself as a fraud and cheater in your forties, despite never having cheated or lied since. No one likes being labelled and judged, yet everyone is guilty of labelling and judging others and themselves, positively and negatively. People with low self-esteem do this because labels serve as security blankets in an unstable world where they don't know who they are or where they stand in life.

The second I left the army and lost my status as a soldier, I hit rock bottom in life because my sense of self totally disintegrated. If I wasn't a soldier, I was nothing, and I chased everything to try to reclaim my sense of self. I worked on building sites, set up my own businesses (all of which flopped), worked at bars as a doorman, and worked in sales and finance, but none of these jobs made me feel as significant as I had as a soldier. Jumping from job to job made me feel worthless, and I knew I didn't want to live a life where I had to stand in line, not think as an individual, play by the rules, and do as I was told, but that was all I knew. Now, without those rules and standards, I was a chaotic, lost shell of a man.

Knowing I wasn't significant made me feel horrible and depressed. I spent hours of my day comparing myself to other people and became more and more crippled by self-hatred as I realised I was nothing more than one of those cowardly and weak civilians I had spent the past eight years looking down on. I ended up in a hole that I didn't know how I'd even gotten into in the first place, let alone knowing how I could get out of it. My self-esteem plummeted to what felt like a point of no return, and that's often the danger of labelling yourself: you get comfortable with the labels.

Whilst it may sound absurd for someone to enjoy feeling

miserable about themselves, there's a reason why so many people refer to themselves as a loser, a nobody, or a failure for decades of their lives: they feel comfortable in doing so; otherwise, they wouldn't call themselves these horrible things. Strangely enough, the reason you berate and chastise yourself is that you take comfort in doing so. The labels you assign yourself, no matter how limiting or negative they may be, give you a strong sense of self, so much so that you will oftentimes find yourself continuing to behave in a way which preserves them. When you've lived two, five, or even ten years of your life abiding by the labels you assign yourself, from depressive to procrastinator or loser, it's scary to imagine life without them.

I've known people who became repeat offenders because their family and society as a whole only saw them as a criminal. I've known people in their late forties who have taken multiple university courses and still only eat pot noodles and live on the cheap because they identify as being a student; I've seen people drop out of life-saving eating-disorder treatment because the treatment threatened their identity as an anorexic; and I've known hundreds of people who have stopped seeking treatment for their depression or anxiety because they're scared of who they'll be if they're cured. There are mothers who don't know what to do with themselves when their children grow up, and there are men who hit forty-five and suddenly trade in their old cars for a sports car in an attempt to reclaim their lost youth. I spent years after the army acting like a soldier on leave. The army culture revolved around working hard and playing harder, which meant I spent all of my free time acting like a fool, getting utterly wasted, and messing around with women I didn't know five to six times a week.

Now let me just clarify this here (before I'm bombarded with defensive emails about how important certain labels are in your life): there's nothing wrong with being something and feeling proud of being that thing, whether that thing is your motherhood, your sexuality, your career role, your dietary choice, your gender, your political alignment, or your religion. You can be proud of yourself for who you are, what you've overcome, what you stand for, and the community you're a part of. The issue arises when you define yourself by these things. A label may be part of who you are, but it's not who you are as a whole. There's more to you than a label, and it's detrimental to your own self-image to minimise your character, likes, dislikes, history, present, values, and soul to a couple of labels which are up for interpretation and evaluation.

Some people may argue you're not Christian or vegan enough, some people may think you act too straight to be gay, some people may say you don't look disabled, and some people will claim that you're naive or evil because of the politics you're associated with. Other people's perceptions of your labels cause you to enter what can be a lifetime cycle of never-ending self-defence and self-clarification with people who don't know you and don't care to know you. The diverse understanding and perception of certain labels lead people to believe that those assigning themselves to those labels should fulfil a particular role in society, but those who don't meet expectations are left feeling obliged to prove their identity and legitimacy of their label. You shouldn't have to explain yourself to anyone in life, but defining yourself by labels puts you in a position where you repeatedly have to.

There is more to you than the labels you assign to yourself, and you are different from every other person out there who also identifies with the same labels you do. Don't hide these parts of yourself, but don't give others the opportunity to jeopardise your feelings of adequacy and self-worth by using your labels to project their prejudices and assumptions onto you. When a label is attacked, misconstrued, and abused by closed-minded and prejudice people, the only people who suffer are those whose selves are tied up in the significance of that label. Don't give away your power to those kinds of people.

DON'T WAIT FOR LIFE TO HAPPEN

It took years of being a fool and failure for me to finally realise my search for a fitting label was leading me down a meaningless and wasteful path. Something needed to change, and I realised it wasn't the world around me that needed to. I was sick of being the man I was, and I couldn't face another day of feeling so rotten and disgusted with myself, so I committed to making a change.

The biggest mistake most people make is that they wait for their life to change. They tell themselves it'll get better when they're thirty years old, when they're forty, when they're fifty, when they're thinner, when they're fitter, when they've dyed their hair a new colour, when their children grow up, or when their boss quits. Yet, at the end of the day, they just sit around waiting for these things to happen. Your life will never change unless you change. You're the deciding factor in your life; you're the thing that's standing in your way and holding you back from feeling more fulfilled, happier, less anxious, and less depressed.

Yes, there are external factors which can help you, like medication, therapy, better environments, and more security, but you have to do the work. No one is going to come in and wave a magic wand and whisper the secret formula to you, and no one is going to make you feel better or take away your flaws and inhibitions. You have to work through them.

Sometimes, things can't be cured or some things won't go away completely, but how you view your life is entirely in your control. How you manage your life and how you emotionally and mentally filter life is entirely up to you, no matter what your inhibitions are. You have autonomy over how you perceive your life and who you are, and only you have the ability to bring about the change you wish to see in yourself. Your dream self-concept will never become an actuality unless you realise the power you have over your fear, depression, low self-image, low self-esteem, and low self-worth. You are the crafter of your image, your outputs, and your drive, so it's time to stop waiting for the world to change you and start being creative with yourself.

CHAPTER ELEVEN

WHO THE HELL ARE YOU THEN?

THERE ARE CURRENTLY HUNDREDS OF EMAILS IN MY inbox from people all worried about the same thing: they don't know who they are or who they want to become. They email me, a perfect stranger, in the hopes that I have the time to get to know them, identify who they are *for* them, and point them in the right direction. Needless to say, I don't respond to these kinds of emails besides a friendly hello and well wishes on their journey of self-development. Why? Because I am self-aware enough to know that no matter how many years I've taught life coaching and no matter how long I talk to someone, I will never be in a position to tell another person who they are.

Listen, if you reach out to a guru, friend, family member, or life coach hoping that they will tell you who you are, and that person gives you an answer, remove them from your life immediately. Anyone who feels they don't know who they are due to their low self-esteem is in a vulnerable position; therefore, anyone with the audacity to give that person a subjective and biased response (which they know will be taken seriously from the questioner) deserves a firm talking to. Nobody, no matter how qualified they are or how well they know you, should tell you who you are, and it's dangerous for you to develop your self-concept off other people's perceptions of you.

Listening and reflecting on criticism and feedback is essential for growth, but taking all feedback as gospel and using it to formulate an accurate reflection of who you are will culminate in you becoming a confused sludge of a person with even less sense of self than you started off with. You should never rely on someone else to tell you who you are or who you should be. Your opinion of yourself needs to be unclouded from external judgment and perspectives. The only way you're ever going to know who you are is by spending some time by yourself in deep self-reflection.

Understanding who you are is like learning about your values: you have to strip yourself naked of everything—appearance, career, achievements, failures, relationships, and religious beliefs—and reflect on what you have left. You may not think there's any more to you than these things you've built your life around, but taking all these external elements away leaves you with your authentic self. Your authentic self is a capsule of memories, values, emotions, feelings, thoughts, creativity, philosophies, and dreams. Unfortunately, you (like most people) don't see those things as valuable; they're mere shadows in comparison to your external factors and real-world status symbols.

When I introduce clients to themselves, I like to demonstrate the complexity of their being by dividing them up into three parts: the body, the mind, and the soul. I'm not a religious person, so I understand why some people find *soul* an uncomfortable word to use, so feel free to pick whatever word feels best to you (*heart* is a popular alternative). To me, the three distinctions break up the following factors of your sense of being: how you are physically in the world, how you think within the world, and how you feel in response to the world and your presence within it. When people ask me how to distinguish between the three parts, I usually refer to a pain analogy. If someone you didn't know were to punch you, you'd feel that pain physically but not so much within yourself; however, if you were to lose a loved one or go through a breakup, the pain you'd feel wouldn't be overtly physical (though over time may manifest as such). The pain of grief and loss may be triggered by thoughts, but this pain isn't felt in the mind but rather somewhere else inside you; grief seems to hurt the very essence of your being.

Your mind and soul have the most significant impact on your life; how they interact can either make your day or destroy your year. Your soul feeds off the thoughts you choose to give attention and energy to, meaning you can spend years of your life suffering from grief, heartache, dissatisfaction, loneliness, and self-hatred should your thoughts remain focused on matters which incite these emotions. Ruminating over all your missed opportunities, former lovers, most painful humiliations, brutal failures, and lost loved ones leaves you feeling drained and heavy with despair.

THE IMPACT YOUR THOUGHTS HAVE ON YOUR HEALTH

Most people believe that they have absolutely no control over their thoughts, and there's *some* truth to that. You can't control all those negative thoughts that suddenly bombard you in bed at 2 am—thoughts come to you spontaneously. Nobody has ever willed themselves to think of distressing, hateful memories and ideas for the fun of it (well, unless they're acting and need to cry for a scene). Whilst it's true that you can't stop any of the thousands of thoughts you have a day, you can *choose* how you respond to them and how much significance you give them. Whether you would like to admit it or not, every time you waste hours of your life dwelling on a negative thought, you do so by choice. No one else forces you to sit on your bed for hours and think about how much of a failure and total waste of space you are—you force yourself to. You allow your mind to churn out of control and run your soul amok and yet, for some bizarre reason, you think losing weight, getting a nose job, having your breasts done, dying your hair, waking up at 6 am, or going to the gym is the solution and makes all these nasty thoughts disappear.

Look, I'm not saying that things like losing weight or getting a nose job are inherently bad; in fact, some are incredibly good for you to do, but when your logic takes you down this path when you're struggling with low self-esteem and worth, it's obvious that your focus is off. There is no use in thinking that by changing your external appearance, it will fix your internal dilemma. You've probably pumped more money, time, and energy into your looks and body than you have into self-development, meditation, mindfulness, and therapy. Your body is important, of course; it's your vehicle and life source, so it demands a level of attention and care in order to function efficiently. However, the amount of energy and time put into it is disproportionate in comparison to how small a role it plays when it comes to mind and soul. Without a healthy soul and mind, the body deteriorates. You become more tired, gain or lose a dangerous amount of weight, eat unhealthy foods, become more distracted and dizzy, feel demotivated and weaker, and (potentially) start developing dangerous health conditions.

As I hope you'll now be able to see, there is a mental and physical danger in not knowing who you are outside of all the external superficialities. Having a superficial relationship with yourself in which you know all about your career, relationship status, appearance, physical flaws, and talents doesn't account for the lack of relationship you have with your authentic self. Neglecting your authenticity not only means you live a lesser life, but also means you deny others your full potential. In a very similar manner to Freud's iceberg theory, which argued that human consciousness exists on three levels (with only one being accessible to the public), your whole sense of being is like an iceberg. Your conscious self, the part of you that you formulate and contrive before putting on display for everyone to see, is just the tip of the iceberg. Your subconscious and unconscious self, however, lie deep beneath the surface, out of sight and out of mind to everyone, including yourself.

People become so comfortable with the performance they're putting on that they're even capable of fooling themselves of their own authenticity and believing their own performance. It takes a lot of courage and self-awareness to step back and ask yourself which parts of your conscious self are authentic and which are being employed to hide the aspects of yourself you don't want others to see. It's healthy and necessary to regularly ask yourself which parts of yourself you willingly show others and which parts you keep hidden before analysing whether or not this arrangement is working for you. Are you hiding your authenticity for the good of others or for the good of yourself, or are you scared to look inside yourself for fear of what you'll find?

THE FABLE OF THE HIDDEN TRUTH

Many centuries ago, there was once a convention that happened in the heavens. The human race was advancing exponentially in both science and technology, so the gods gathered together to express their concerns about being discovered. They were terrified that the human race would one day become so advanced that they'd realise their own potential and power, resulting in the gods becoming obsolete. The head god called the meeting to begin and requested any suggestions from the floor as to how the gods could keep humans ignorant to their potential and help them remain necessary. One god stepped up to the podium and suggested that they hide human truth at the very top of the highest mountain, where no human could reach.

Whilst the gods seemed pleased with this idea, a little god stepped forward and burst their bubble. 'The humans are becoming too advanced', he stated. 'There's a high chance they'll be capable of building an apparatus to help them breathe at the top of a mountain. We cannot risk putting it there.'

Upon hearing this, the gods became frustrated and began thinking carefully once more. 'How about', another god piped up, 'we bury it deep at the bottom of the ocean? No human will ever be able to breathe underwater; they can't possibly get down there!'

The gods cheered and applauded in admiration at this response, but the little god stepped forward meekly and raised his hand. 'I hate to burst your bubble', he said, 'but at the rate they're going, there's a good chance the humans will be able to build a vehicle which can take them deep underwater. We can't possibly take that risk either.'

The gods had started to become sick of the little god's know-it-all attitude, so they turned the pressure onto him.

'Alright, wise one', the chief god roared sarcastically, 'if you're so clever, why don't you come up with a solution? Where are we supposed to hide the truth of human potential if you think they're so advanced?'

'Simple', the little god replied as he stepped up to the podium to address the court. 'We hide the truth inside of them; it's the one place they never look. They're so busy looking outside of themselves for happiness that they never turn inwards to reflect upon their own resources. That's the safest place to hide the truth.'

THE QUALITY OF YOUR RELATIONSHIPS DETERMINES THE QUALITY OF YOUR LIFE

Some people feel the pressure to hide their authenticity from their family, friends, and society for fear of being hated, abused, rejected, attacked, judged, shunned, disliked, unloved, and unaccepted, but you deserve to live your life fully. Life is short: be yourself. Find out where you belong, and find those who truly accept you for who are, unfiltered and unashamed. If you live a life disconnected from yourself, this disconnect will propagate into your other relationships. People spend their lives faking who they are in order to fit in with other inauthentic people. You live and breathe a society of inauthenticity: everyone is fake to themselves and to each other to the point that no one knows where they truly stand with anyone. Why? Because everyone is terrified of rejection.

It may feel easy and comfortable to fit in with others, even at the cost of your authenticity, but the quality of your life is dependent upon the quality of your relationships. You can't expect people to trust you if you don't have enough trust and faith in yourself to be authentic. Yes, people can and will reject you for your authentic self, but there will also be those who love and accept you, and those are the only people who matter. Authenticity demands that you are true to who you are, which means your energy shouldn't be wasted on pleasing other people or focusing on whether people like you or not. Nobody can take anything away from you or add anything to you, so you don't have to base your self-esteem and value on other people's validation or disapproval.

You may change careers in the next few years, lose your family, get a divorce, move to a different country, or take up a new hobby. The status of your health may change, you may pick up some bad habits and drop some old ones, your attitude and outlook on life may take a 180-degree turn, and your life ambitions may change completely. Many things in your life can change, but there's only one thing that will always remain the same: who you are at your core. This is why it's so crucial that you take the time to identify who you are at your core and embrace it with your whole being. You have the potential to be the only constant you have in life, so don't let yourself down.

CHAPTER TWELVE

[YOUR NAME HERE] VERSUS THE WORLD

HOW MANY PEOPLE DO YOU FOLLOW ONLINE WHO YOU think are better than you? You most likely follow thousands of people online (either on Facebook, Twitter, YouTube, or Instagram), all of whom you think are better than you in some way: better bodies, jobs, lifestyles, looks, sense of fashion, Instagram feeds, wit, opportunities, holidays, or mental health. You follow these people because you admire what they have, what they've achieved, and who they are in some way, but you're also conscious that the mindless, endless scrolling on social media leaves you feeling depressed and uninspired.

Yet, despite how it makes you feel, you continue to spend hours a day scrolling through pictures of people who make you feel lesser than. It's as though you're addicted to envy and self-flagellation: seeing all these beautiful, happy, and colourful posts only makes you feel more insecure and stuck in your comparatively bland, poor, and un-Instagrammable life. There are two possible reasons why you continue to engage in this emotionally exhausting behaviour. It's either because (a) you wish to live vicariously through them, whilst doing little to nothing to improve and better your own circumstances, or (b) you want to witness their downfall or fall to grace, that is, the moment they gain weight, lose the money, age horrendously, or break up with their partner. Unfortunately, *schadenfreude* is a common thing, and there are many people out there who wait patiently for something to bring another person down a peg or two so that they join the provincial realm of misery.

THE THREE LEVELS OF SELF-COMPARISON

There are three levels to self-comparison: (a) judging whether or not someone is better than you, (b) judging whether they're the same as you, or (c) judging whether they are worse off than you. Most people are unaware of how quickly they are to judge others, but being judgmental is an instinctual part of human nature, so much so that you will (unconsciously) analyse people you meet or walk past on the street. Even in a brief glance, you will compare yourself to another person to determine whether they are taller, stronger, weaker, fatter, thinner, richer, poorer, less attractive, or more attractive than you. You've probably even caught yourself in the act of thinking someone has nicer hair than you do or passed someone who you think has an awful sense of style.

The second you see someone, you compare yourself to them on a very primitive level, usually unconsciously. However, the more you know someone, the deeper your comparison against them becomes, as you begin to analyse whether they are more educated, grew up wealthier, have a better salary, or live in a nicer home. What's worse, the more insecure you are about yourself, the more conscious your comparison becomes.

I was twenty-eight years old when I reentered education: not majorly old but considerably older than my sixteen- and eighteen-year-old classmates (mentally, at least). Turns out, teenage boys can be irritating know-it-alls with frustrating superiority complexes. Every time a group of boys found out I didn't get an A in a mock exam they all easily aced, I was mocked for being so much older yet dumber than they were. I had to remind myself within the moment that I shouldn't expect much more from them; these kids had a much narrower mindset. They had sheltered lives, they didn't know what the real world was like, and they certainly hadn't spent eight years working in the army, as I had. To them, the mark of superiority and success in life was an A grade, so, according to their standards, they were winning at life majorly. If they were already beating a twenty-eight-year-old man, they were definitely going to sail through life, no problem. This mindset is what leads to the downfall of so many people. Many individuals spend the first chunk of their lives striving to succeed within a pre-constructed climate of grades, clubs, and playground popularity standards, only to be slapped in the face by the chaotic reality of the unstructured and fluctuating culture of our real society.

I was, thankfully, in a place in life at that time where I didn't feel any need or desire to prove myself to youngsters. I knew my level of intelligence, and I knew I was on a journey of self-improvement. I didn't care about impressing kids with my grades. People with low self-confidence and low self-esteem can sometimes take joy or comfort in seeing others fail or struggle, and I was self-aware enough to recognise that I was providing that service to these kids. Those kinds of people need some kind of ego boost to make themselves feel bigger, and there will be plenty of people in your life who use you the same way. As someone with low self-esteem, you likely pride yourself on being a good, non-judgmental person. You're probably a people pleaser who tries to be friends with everyone, so you could never imagine being someone who feels joy from people's misfortunes and downfalls. Sure, you may not be someone who is unkind and who consciously belittles and harshly criticises people, but if you're someone who compares yourself to others (albeit in a complimentary way), you undoubtedly compare yourself to others in a way which boosts your own ego.

THE DOUBLE-EDGED SWORD OF SELF-COMPARISON

Now, I'm not implying you're a bad person for doing this; it's just the nature of comparison. If you compare yourself to others in one way (e.g., comparing yourself to someone superior to you), you will, naturally, compare yourself to others in the other two ways I described at the beginning of this chapter. Comparison doesn't exist in sections; it exists as a whole: you can't pick and choose what kind of comparison you engage with. There is no need to feel ashamed about comparing yourself. Most people compare themselves to others, both positively and negatively, which is why society thrives and profits from the comparison complex.

People compare themselves to celebrities all the time and want to emulate them so much that they'll go out of their way to buy the clothes they wear, watch the shows they're in, or go as far as having plastic surgery to look like them. Daytime television thrives off comparison. America and Britain have very similar television shows that epitomise humanity's guilty delight in judgment and *schadenfreude*: *The Jerry Springer Show*, *Dr. Phil*, and *The Jeremy Kyle Show*. These tabloid talk shows (often referred to as trash TV) showcase the lurid and disgraceful personal lives of underprivileged, working-class, and underclass individuals for public entertainment. From marital affairs to incest, drug abuse, sexually transmitted infections, rape, and child abuse, these shows sensationalise the misfortunate and lamentable lives of those the societal system has overlooked, neglected, and cast aside. Despite our natural aversion to melodrama, conflict, and scandal in our real lives, these shows are immensely popular, garnering millions of views every day. Most people wouldn't want to associate with anyone from these television shows; they wouldn't want to talk to them personally, hang out with them, or get involved in their complicated lives, yet they're willing to do so through the medium of television. Millions of people are eager to spend time with these people at a distance, laughing at or gossiping about their misfortune despite having no interest in them on a deeper, meaningful level.

So, why are people so addicted to watching these kinds of shows if they wouldn't enjoy this kind of energy in their personal lives? Simple: these shows make them feel good about themselves. People with low self-esteem feel awful about themselves; they consider themselves the lowest of the low, pathetic creatures who can't do anything right in life, with no friends, no future, and no hope. But then they find television shows dedicated to humiliating and degrading people whose lives are so destructive and ruined that it makes the viewer's life look amazing in comparison.

People are always looking for validation that they're not fundamentally fucked up and that they're doing something right in life, so tabloid shows fulfil that need by feeding into people's impulsive and intrinsic need for comparison. It's a dirty and exploitative business model for both viewers and participants who are always vulnerable people. The good news is that *The Jeremy Kyle Show* was permanently cancelled in the United Kingdom as of 2019, but this long-overdue executive decision was unfortunately triggered by the suicide of one of the show's contestants.

On the other side of the spectrum, I once had a mentor who I totally idolised. He'd played such a huge role in my life during the first few years I started studying counselling, and this man was practically godlike to me; he could do no wrong. One day, he asked me to accompany him to a conference he was speaking at and to join him on stage during his speech. Naturally, I accepted with honour. My idol, a guy who was admired and followed by thousands of people, had chosen me to learn from him personally and get a glimpse of his life behind the curtain. I was so pepped up and excited about the day that I hardly slept for weeks; I couldn't stop fantasising about all the insight and industry secrets I'd learn from him (perhaps he'd even give me a few personal tips and legs up). The day, however, didn't pan out the way I'd hoped it would. It wasn't because my mentor wasn't amazing, because he was. Actually, that was the issue. The second he got up on stage and started talking, the colour drained from my face. He was absolutely phenomenal. I literally paled in comparison to him. There was no way, I thought, that I could ever be as good as him. He was something else; he was beyond anything I could be on a really amazing day. My mood immediately plummeted. My low self-esteem had gotten the better of me.

There are only two main directions comparison can take you: you can gain a sense of false confidence by comparing yourself to those you deem lesser than, or you can allow yourself to feel voided and nullified by a sense of shame and inadequacy when admiring those better than you. Neither, obviously, are helpful. The outcomes of comparison are fundamentally warped by pride, naivety, ignorance, and unkindness, either to others or yourself. People who are secure in who they are don't need to analyse other people in order to place themselves in the world, and they aren't affected by those who try to put them down. Also, their ability to maintain a healthy relationship with themselves outside the context of judgment means that other people's successes, advantages, or disadvantages don't affect their perception of their own worth.

THE FEAR OF NOT BEING 'GOOD ENOUGH'

If anything in this chapter has resonated with you, the most probable reason why you may be addicted to comparison is that you don't believe you are good enough. You listen to your insecurities and tell yourself you're inherently incapable of achieving or doing certain things in life, even if you've been successful or proven yourself wrong a thousand times. I once had a client who was obsessed with getting promoted at work; in fact, the chance for promotion was the reason he woke up every day. Yet, despite having been promoted several times throughout multiple companies over the last thirty years of his life, he still suffered from imposter syndrome. He was terrified of being caught and called out for being a fraud. He never felt like he was good enough for the roles he was given, but he kept chasing every opportunity that came up, in the hopes that one day he'd chase this feeling away and prove himself wrong. On the other hand, from my own personal experience, every promotion I got from the army meant I was good enough. I was in a place in life where I needed that external validation, because I wasn't a free being and secure enough within myself to acknowledge my own value and significance in this world. Both men in these examples are chasing the same thing for the same fundamental need to feel good enough, and whilst their responses to the results were different, the fragile and unstable ground they mentally stood upon was the same.

Generating your own idea of self-worth can be terrifying. It's much easier and less stressful to measure yourself according to other people's standards than your own because you can pass blame and responsibility when you fall short of other people's expectations. Telling yourself you're not good enough is a perfect excuse for never trying in life. *'There's no point applying for that job, I'm not good enough'. 'There's no point taking up that sport, I'll never be good enough'. 'There's no point trying to set up my own business, I'm not good enough'.*

Stop leaning on your excuses in life and start valuing yourself and your full potential. Just because you're imperfect doesn't mean you're not good enough; just because you're bad at something now doesn't mean you're not good enough; just because your parents rejected you or you got dumped by the love of your life doesn't mean you're not good enough. Stop giving your power away and stop measuring yourself against other people's standards. There will be people who reject you in life, but you need to learn how to be OK with who you are first and foremost and accept this rejection as part of life. Just because someone rejects you doesn't mean your value or significance as an individual is diminished.

CHAPTER THIRTEEN

HOW YOUR 'SELF' IS GETTING IN YOUR WAY

HAVE YOU EVER FELT LIKE THERE'S A BATTLE GOING on in your mind, as though there are multiple parts of yourself telling you very different stories about who you are and what you're capable of? Throughout my years of working as a personal-growth mentor, I've become familiar with the three ways people come to terms with the self, which is divided into their self-worth, self-esteem, and self-concept. These three parts of the self are what your head is battling against every day. When suffering from low self-confidence, these three concepts rage a constant battle in your mind, and when you're in a bad mental space already, it's hard to rationally decipher which one you should focus on building, which one you *need* to work on first, or figure out what is the difference between the three.

Each facet of the self is important, but most people tend to prioritise self-esteem over everything else; 'how to build your self-esteem' is searched for far more on Google than 'self-value' and 'self-concept' are, which makes sense theoretically:

self-esteem is important, and developing strong self-esteem is crucial for living a mature and emotionally stable life. But self-esteem relates solely to how you feel about your external self; it stems from the impression you think you make on others (i.e., how you think they perceive you in terms of your behaviour, appearance, and interactions).

Naturally, self-esteem is highly dependent upon the quality of things you produce, from your career to your children, physique, and talents. However, the danger of drawing validation from external factors is that your esteem becomes determined by fluxing elements. Chasing self-esteem, therefore, becomes an exhausting and unsustainable way of living. It seems like for every success that boosts your confidence, there are twenty failures solidly knocking you back down to rock bottom. Then, when you start conceiving imperfections, failures, and rejections as markers of who you are, your self-esteem takes a harsh battering, and the more you spend days of your life comparing yourself to others, the more your self-esteem plummets. But the reason you focus so much on improving your self-esteem is that your self-esteem is on the frontline; when something goes wrong, it's the thing that gets impacted first, usually with a critical blow.

Because it's always in the firing line, you (understandably) want to spend all your time and energy repairing and strengthening your self-esteem: it's the armour you wear, it's what people notice about you, and it's what attracts people to (or deters people from) you. But what you don't realise is that your self-esteem is the product of your self-worth, and if you don't look at amending your self-worth, you're never going to fix the issues you have with your self-esteem. Tackling issues of self-esteem before tackling those of self-worth is like going to the gym to lose weight without confronting and changing your diet. Sure, you'll lose a little weight and tone up a bit, but after a while, you'll find yourself plateauing, and you'll become frustrated that you aren't seeing bigger and more significant changes for the amount of exercise you're doing. You can only tackle a symptom for so long, but you won't see long-lasting benefits until you confront the cause of an issue.

RECOGNISING YOUR WORTH

I've already covered a lot about self-worth in chapter nine by discussing how to value yourself based on who you are fundamentally rather than what you do in life. Self-worth is what you believe is your intrinsic value, which doesn't always accurately reflect who you are at the core and who you are willing to be. Your self-worth is based on your understanding of your true, authentic identity and, therefore, can only be built on the facts of who you are.

The value you place on yourself depends on your upbringing and whether or not you were brought up in a home where you were encouraged to grow and learn from your failures or were constantly put down for them. However, even if you recognise that you grew up in an environment which didn't nurture you as it should have and put you down more than it ever built you up, your past doesn't excuse you for clinging onto your low self-worth today. You can identify that your mother belittled you or that your father was emotionally hostile; you can identify that you have trust issues, emotional dysfunction disorder, or complex PTSD because of your upbringing, but these factors are not definitive. They are the emotional leftovers of your childhood, but they do not define you. They are not states you are permanently chained to in life, nor are they stipulations you need to live by, and they don't need to be part of your future unless you allow them to be.

The past does not define you: you determine who you are today through the thoughts you choose to give weight to, the actions you take, and the decisions you make. Other people may have been responsible for the hurt they caused you in the past, but only you are responsible for the pain you carry today. You can't blame your mother or father for the issues you have in your thirties or sixties; they may have triggered the existence of the issue, but the maintenance of it is your responsibility to manage.

You can point the blame at whoever you want to in life, but you *know* that person can't undo what they've done to you; they can't turn back the clocks, and they can't take the pain away as though they were a magician who is the only one who can reverse the curse they placed on you all those years ago. Once the damage is done, it's done, and even if they apologise for what they did and make it up to you, the healing is your responsibility. When a bee stings you, do you expect the bee to come back and heal that sting, or do you expect your body to do its job and heal itself? The same goes for mental and emotional wounds; you can't expect the perpetrators or the triggers to undo what they did or take away the pain: you just have to manage the healing yourself.

GROWING YOUR VALUE

Taking responsibility for the emotional pain you've felt over the years and taking lessons from your experience is how your value grows. Your value develops out of the value-based decisions and actions you take in life; it blossoms from you living transparently, authentically, and openly. Your past will shape your actions, but it is your responsibility to ensure those actions are positive rather than negative.

The people, events, and circumstances of your past are like farmers. Farmers can plant seeds, but they cannot force those seeds to grow. No one forced you to believe in yourself so little, nobody has forced you to define your value by your successes in life, and nobody has forced you to feel as worthless as you do. Only you force yourself to feel the way you do. Out of all the seeds the farmers sowed, you chose to nurture and grow the negative ones. Now it's time to take back control and realise that just because a farmer planted that seed, you don't have to allow it to grow. You can choose which seeds grow, which means you don't have to nurture and grow every seed a farmer plants in your brain. In fact, you have the power to only nurture and grow the seeds sowed by positive influences, positive life experiences, kind words, and good people. As for those negative plants you've spent your whole life nurturing—the ones which have sucked all your energy and self-worth for years, potentially decades—it's time to let those die. They're a waste of air, and they're not benefitting your life in any shape or form.

DEVELOPING A SELF-CONCEPT

Although most people just want quick answers or how-to guides for fixing the parts of themselves they're uncomfortable with, there aren't any techniques, steps, or processes that can help you accept who you are at the core. Discovering and accepting your self-worth demands that you commit to a lifelong journey of growth, extending yourself to others, sharing your value, taking responsibility for your emotional and mental inconsistencies, and embracing your imperfections. Nobody in the world can make you feel better about yourself. There isn't a magic book, course, guru, or life coach who has the secrets to your eternal fulfilment and self-acceptance. Why? Because there's nothing wrong with you; there aren't any missing links, emotional diseases, or cognitive miswirings. The only problem you have is that you haven't learned how to manage your thoughts, master your emotions, or free yourself from the opinions and judgment of others. In other words, you've spent too much of your life worrying about how you relate to others (i.e., your self-esteem) instead of focusing on how you relate to yourself (i.e., your self-worth).

You're probably wondering where the third idea, self-concept, comes into the equation. Self-concept, like self-esteem, is something people pre-emptively concern themselves with, and understandably so. When you have self-hatred and low self-esteem, it's refreshing and liberating to daydream about being a totally different person in a few years' time: an amazing, super-healthy, career-driven, rich, helpful, popular, intelligent, and well-travelled individual who is happy within themselves and has an amazing life filled with wonderful relationships.

Self-conception is an idealised vision of yourself: the person you wish you could possibly and eventually become. If you don't have a self-conception to work towards, you end up not trying anything in life, which, in turn, propagates ideas of low self-worth and low self-esteem. People with no self-conception are those who were never taught how to positively visualise themselves in the future. However, those who have a self-concept but no self-worth tend to find their self-concept gnaws away at their self-esteem. Many people have lofty self-concepts of their future selves, yet very few commit to becoming that person by taking action today and changing their attitudes, behaviours, or habits in order to develop into that person. Instead, they all secretly hope they can skip out on all the hard work and just transform overnight thanks to a new job, a new look, a new partner, a new home, a new body, or even just a new age.

I once coached a former soldier who had spent the last few years of his life trying to establish his own personal training business. The problem was, his lifestyle choices were undesirable and weren't serving him well. Like I had years before, he had fallen into using drugs and alcohol and was struggling through what seemed to be an on-and-off relapse-and-recovery cycle. He would manage to stay sober for a few months and build up a loyal clientele base, but then exaggerate to others about how well his business was doing. He would exaggerate the number of clients he had and the number of hours he worked just to impress other people, but when he finally admitted to himself that he wasn't doing as well as he should, he would turn to drugs and alcohol to numb the feelings of shame and worthlessness. Naturally, his drug and alcohol habit began to interfere with his work and clients, which he lost over time, leaving him back at square one.

He, like many others, came to me asking for help with self-esteem because that's what he perceived was the problem. Hopefully, this example has once again demonstrated that the issue at hand was fundamentally his self-concept and self-worth, not his self-esteem. If he had high self-worth, he wouldn't have abused drugs and alcohol the way he was. He also wouldn't have needed to mask this shame and instability during his periods of sobriety by inflating his ego, exaggerating his success and lying about a lifestyle he couldn't live up to (at the moment). His low self-worth was blinding him from the realisation that what he dreamed of having could be a reality if he would only be patient and honest about his current circumstances. The shame he felt about his current lifestyle compared to his ideal circumstances sent him spiralling into a cycle of deception and relapse; but if he had recognised how intrinsically valuable he was, he wouldn't have needed to feel ashamed and would be ready and willing to grow into the person he dreamed of becoming.

THE GAP BETWEEN WHO YOU ARE AND WHO YOU WANT TO BE

People with low self-esteem usually fall into this cycle of chasing their idealised self rather than working on the issues they're struggling with because their self-concept is the happier and more successful version. Unfortunately, the gaping void between who they are today and who they want to be can be overwhelming for people with low self-esteem due to their *fixed-mind construct* (as Carol Dweck called it). For example, you can have dreams of earning a lot of money, but when you see your bank account and debts, you become incredibly depressed and feel it's not worth working all the extra overtime. Or you may have a self-concept which focuses on losing weight and having a certain figure, but when you see the stagnation in your progress or you notice you aren't progressing as quickly as other people, you feel defeated and unmotivated to try anymore.

The stark difference between who a person is and who a person wants to become usually triggers destructive behaviours in those with low self-esteem, which aren't always related to drugs and alcohol; some people start starving themselves or binge-eat, whilst others over-exercise, spend excessive amounts of money on a regular basis, go gambling, engage in unhealthy sexual behaviours, and so on. In other words, these people will take any major yet short-term fix to feel happier and escape the claustrophobic feelings of failure and self-loathing.

In order to achieve growth and fulfilment, you need to break free from this dream of happiness and reject all drives for it. Happiness will not move you forward in life towards your ideal self-concept; it won't help you grow or help you progress in any field of your life. Your self-concept may seem far off, but it will never come into fruition unless you commit to who you are and accept that your worth today is just as great as it would ever be in the future, even with a different career, lifestyle, and income. Your ideal self is no more worthy, no more valuable, and no more important than who you are right now. By all means, commit to working towards becoming your ideal self; learn and do whatever you can every day to move forward and just strive to be a better person than you were yesterday. You know the dangers of comparing yourself to other people, but it can be equally dangerous to compare yourself to your ideal self if you idolise it too much. You are more than capable of becoming the person you've always dreamed of becoming, but you'll never become that person if you don't recognise you're already worthy enough right now in this moment.

CHAPTER FOURTEEN

BUSTING THE CONFIDENCE MYTH

SOME BELIEVE THAT CONFIDENCE IS SOMETHING people are born with. Whilst I'm not here to tell you what or what not to believe in, I'd like to encourage you to accept the idea that confidence is a trait which can be adopted by anyone, regardless of their innate idiosyncrasies. There may be some people in this world who seem to be born confident; they were confident babies who grew up into confident, extroverted adults, but that's not to say confidence is an exclusively genetic trait. You are not a victim of circumstance; when the universe was handing out genetics for confidence, they didn't skip you because you're not worthy of it. You can learn how to be confident, regardless of whether you're introverted or extroverted.

I receive a lot of emails from people asking for tips, tricks, and techniques for developing their confidence because blogs, videos, and online gurus claim that confidence is a skill which can be learned, as though it's like taking up graphic design, tap dancing, or singing. My take on confidence is slightly controversial, as it goes against everything everyone else preaches about its accessibility: I don't regard confidence as a skill. Rather, I consider confidence a way of being; it's a mindset, and mindsets are very different from skills. Mindsets aren't learned; they're developed through self-acceptance and self-compassion. Sure, you can learn how to meditate, but inner peace and tranquillity won't come automatically with the art of meditation alone. It develops as you apply meditation and mindfulness techniques throughout your day in different aspects of your life. It's a bit like doing one hundred crunches every day expecting to get abs. You can learn how to do crunches, and you can put in a lot of hard work to do a hundred crunches but still won't see any results, even after six months. This is because abs aren't developed from doing crunches alone; they're developed through a varied weight-training programme, a healthy diet, and cardio. Building abs (or any muscle group) isn't a skill; it's the result of a culmination of different activities and skills that have been committed to over an extensive period of time. In my opinion, this is how confidence is developed. You can't just focus on doing one thing and becoming really good at that thing in the hopes that confidence will develop out of your commitment to it. You need to culminate a multitude of processes (behaviours, thoughts, and actions) which will help you progress towards its development.

Jim Rohn (one of my heroes growing up) once said, 'Look, if you want things to change, YOU have to change. If you change, everything will change for you. Don't wait for things to change.' Everything begins with you: who you are and how you think is entirely within your realm of control. Things and people can try to influence you, but only you are responsible for passing that power over to these external factors. This is why it's useless to blame other people and circumstances for your shortcomings, failures, or misfortunes in life. Whilst external factors out of your control will impact you, the only things that truly influence your actions and outputs in life are the beliefs you have about yourself. If you believe you're competent, skilled, and talented, then you'll feel confident about yourself; but if you believe you're worthless, unemployable, miserable, untalented, and hopeless, you'll never be confident. You can change your looks, your job, your body, your relationship, your hobbies, your friends, or your hometown, but what really needs changing are the beliefs you have about yourself.

THE STAGES TO DEVELOPING CONFIDENCE

To develop confidence, you need to stop focussing on how the outside world makes you feel about yourself and start focusing on how you work from the inside out, that is, how your thoughts influence your feelings, how your feelings influence your actions (or inactions), and how your actions or inactions impact your outcomes. If you want to become successful in life, you must become 100 percent secure in who you are, because progress is dependent upon a sustainable stream of confidence and self-assurance. In order to understand more about the complexities of confidence (and why it can't simply be learned), we need to break it down and explore the three realms it's comprised of. Confidence consists of:

1. Belief in your own competence
2. Belief in your ability to learn and solve problems
3. Belief in your own self-worth (i.e., your intrinsic value)

These three realms are pretty straightforward to unpack, but I'll elaborate on them briefly. A lack of belief in one's competency leads people to question whether they're good enough as partners, parents, or employees. Lack of belief in one's ability to learn and solve problems holds people back from standing up for themselves, going for a new job or promotion, taking up a new hobby (or returning to an old one), going on to higher education, or studying for an exam. Sometimes a person's lack of belief in their ability to learn stems from the education systems they went through. Educational institutions have very specific ways in which they expect people to learn and demonstrate knowledge, which overlooks the fact that most people don't learn in the same way. In fact, there are four different learning styles and each type responds best to different methods of teaching. The four styles of learning include visual, auditory, reading and writing, and kinaesthetic. Those who aren't best suited to learning through reading and writing tend to not do as well in school as those who are, so these children are labelled as weaker students by their teachers and the system as a whole. Because the system told them they're inferior, these children grow up to believe they're not capable of learning, and they lower their self-worth according to these systematic standards.

I was one of these children. For as long as I can remember, I was a talker, meaning in school I was a little chatterbox, and my teacher, Mrs Payne, hated me for it. Her biggest complaint to my parents was that I wouldn't keep quiet in my seat during class. It was only when I hit adulthood that I realised I am an auditory learner; I learn best when reciting information back to people. If I don't understand something, I need to discuss it with someone, and if I want to teach someone something, I teach them orally. However, I wasted my childhood and teenage years believing I was unintelligent because I chose to believe what that teacher told me. She told me I was a bad student, so I chose to believe her and acted accordingly. I stopped caring about school, I stopped trying to impress people by studying or doing my homework, I became cheeky, I talked back, and I lost out on learning what I could, all because I believed what other people believed of me.

The same can't be said for Gillian. At the age of seven, Gillian (who had earned the nickname Wigglebottom by her teachers) was taken by her mother to see a doctor. Because of the complaints and concerns expressed by her teachers regarding Gillian's fidgetiness, Gillian's mother was worried that her daughter had a learning disorder. She had been advised by the teachers, who were exasperated and worn out by Gillian's behaviour, to see a child psychiatrist and have her officially diagnosed.

When she arrived at the doctor's, little Gillian was guided down a long, dark corridor to a stale-looking room with a dark and worn leather sofa. Conscious that she was being examined for her behaviour, Gillian clamped up with fear and made an exerted effort to sit rigidly stiff with her hands tucked under her legs. The doctor became perplexed. Having heard about Gillian's case from her parents, he found it impossible to diagnose her in her contrary state, so he asked if he could speak to Gillian's mother privately in another room. However, he promised Gillian that he didn't want her to feel afraid or alone, so he turned on the radio to amuse her in their absence. Within seconds, Gillian was left all alone in the musty, stale room. For a while, she remained stiff and seated, as many children would when in a foreign and authoritative place. But then a song came on which Gillian loved. At once, she sprang up off the sofa and began twirling around the room, dancing excitedly to her beloved tune. The doctor and her mother, who were watching from a window, broke into a smile. 'There's nothing wrong with your daughter, Madam', the doctor said as he turned to Gillian's mother. 'She's a dancer.'

The only prescription Gillian got sent home with that day was one for a dance class, any dance class of her choice. Gillian chose ballet. After her first class at dance school, she rushed out excitedly and flung herself into her mother's arms. 'Everyone was like me!' she told her mother excitedly. They needed to move to be able to think. It was wonderful! By the age of ten, Gillian won a scholarship to the Royal Academy of Dance. Over the years, Gillian flourished in her ballet classes. She went on to have a career working for the Royal Opera House, the Royal Shakespeare Company, and the English National Theatre, and danced in many West End and Broadway shows. Whilst her dancing career was prolific, Gillian went on to become a choreographer who just so happened to have one particular fan, a man called Andrew Lloyd Webber, who approached her one day and asked if she would choreograph a new show he had in production. It was called *Cats*.

This young woman, who was once at risk as being labelled by professionals and authorities as an unteachable and misbehaving child, went on to transform the world of musical theatre and become a millionairess all because somebody took the time to look at her and realise she was more complex than the system thought she was. She could have been battered to the ground emotionally and mentally by those in authority who wanted to dismiss her for not fitting into their box, but she had the confidence to create her own opportunities despite what others thought of her.

DON'T BE EMBARRASSED TO ADMIT YOU'RE A NOVICE

Many people waste their lives beating themselves up for not being a particular way or for not doing something with their lives. But it's only once you start building confidence in your self-worth that you free yourself from being obsessed with what you do and what you look like and just start focusing on being a good enough person to others and yourself. Sure, you can strive to be skilled and talented in certain things, but unless you change your beliefs about who you are, you'll always be limited and torn down by your inner critic. Without confidence in your self-worth, you'll never feel truly confident in any aspect of your life, regardless of how secure or knowledgeable you are in a particular field. You may know you're incredibly skilled at your job and that you have all the right qualifications and experience, but unless you're confident in your intrinsic value, you'll always suffer from imposter syndrome. You can be in a long-term, loving, and committed relationship, but without confidence in your intrinsic value, you'll always be paranoid that your partner will leave you or cheat on you.

You probably waste so much energy worrying about what other people think of you and what other people are doing: 'Will my colleagues think I'm antisocial if I don't go to the party?' 'Will people think I look fat in this?' 'Did that person gain weight?' 'Were those people laughing at me when I came into the room?' 'Did that person just subtweet about me?' Caring what other people think of you is a surefire way to waste your life and hold yourself back from being who you truly are. Say you were to start weight training, but you're embarrassed because all the other weightlifters around you are lifting twenty-kilogram dumbbells and you can only lift four kilograms. You can either get embarrassed that you can only lift four kilograms (because it makes you look like you're weak), try to lift ten-kilogram weights and cause yourself serious injury, or you can accept that you're weak. Of course you're weak; you've never done this before. No one is capable of walking into a weight room, having never done any heavy lifting in their life, and find that they're magically capable of benching forty kilograms on their first try. There's nothing to be ashamed of. Everyone starts out weak. The only people who stay weak are those who never try. Who cares if other people in the gym think you're physically weaker than they are? For starters, if they're lifting twenty-kilogram dumbbells, they're probably right. What's wrong with that, and why does it matter to you what they think?

No one is perfect, and no one gets through life without starting at square one. Can square one feel embarrassing at times? Of course. I initially felt embarrassed when I went back to school in my twenties, but I knew that if I didn't go back to school, I wouldn't get the qualifications I needed. I couldn't let embarrassment or pride get in the way of accepting that I needed to do something later in life, so I didn't. Now I run my own business and have developed online courses which are studied across the globe.

You won't ever reach your end goals in life if you expect unquestionable and immaculate results from yourself. Embracing your shortfalls or inferiorities in life is the only way you can develop mastery and expertise. You have to accept that you're weak to become strong, you have to accept your ignorance to become smarter, and you have to accept your naivety to become wiser; otherwise, you'll live the life you've always lived: fixed tightly to your unhappy comfort zone.

IT'S NOT SELFISH TO PRIORITISE YOUR STORY

As for other people's judgmental opinions: the majority don't care nearly as much as you think they do. You may get a passing glance from a stranger for wearing that daring new outfit, but that person will forget you within milliseconds of passing you. You may get someone eyeing up your workout in the gym, but they will forget you as soon as they start working out themselves. If you want to order a burger, but your health-conscious friend only ordered the side salad for dinner, she really won't care or judge you for ordering that burger with fries (and even if she *does*, she'll forget what you ordered within an hour or two).

There are always going to be judgmental, negative people who will gossip, spread rumours, and belittle you. These people are called jerks, and you don't need to appease or be liked by jerks in life. Hell, you shouldn't even *want* to be. You can't be liked by everyone anyway, so if you meet or experience someone unfairly judging you for what you wear, how you do what you do, or how you live your life, be grateful that the trash just took itself out. These aren't people you want to associate with in life, and the more emotional, mental, and physical distance you can have from them, the better.

Your primary concern in life should be how *you're* feeling, what *you're* thinking, what *you're* doing, and why *you're* doing what you're doing. This isn't a selfish disposition; it's a sensible one. Flight attendants don't instruct you to put on your own oxygen mask first before assisting others to put on theirs because the instructions are written by selfish and self-absorbed people. They tell you to put on your own oxygen mask first because they know you won't be of any use to anyone unless you ensure your own safety first. The same goes for self-validation and self-acceptance. How can you ever expect to be accepted, loved, respected, or inspiring if you don't accept, love, respect, or inspire yourself?

You may think it's your weight, looks, income, family, friends, partner, or circumstance which is holding you back from becoming confident, but really, all that's holding you back are your doubts and deep-rooted insecurities about who you are. You're different from everyone else around you, and that difference terrifies you. You can't bear the idea of being outcast, ignored, or rejected, so you live a life shackled to a projection of yourself, one which fits neatly into other people's boxes.

Everyone has a past; everyone has messed up and learned lessons in different ways. Your story might not be a great one; it may be filled with things you're not proud of, people who've hurt you, or people you've hurt. However, whatever your story is, you have to claim it. No, this doesn't mean claiming your story as a victim, because claiming your story as a victim means making your story part of someone else's story rather than keeping it as an entity entirely of its own worth. You can't learn from being part of someone else's story, and you can't learn from trying to live or fit into someone else's story; you can only learn from your own. This is what it means to be unconditionally self-accepting.

Most people believe that how other people treat them reflects who they are. If they're treated badly, they are bad, if they're treated well, they were either good or someone just didn't know they were bad. If people laugh at them, they believe they're a joke. And if people spread gossip about them, they think they're pathetic and unlikeable. If this is how you think, it's time to break free from the lies you have told yourself all these years. You've allowed people who don't have your best interest at heart to convince you that their opinions matter more, that their opinions are more valuable, and that their opinions accurately reflect who you are as a person. You allowed other people to make you feel uncomfortable in your own skin and allowed them to make you question who you are and doubt what you're capable of.

Confidence is about becoming comfortable with your story and with who you are today, regardless of all external opinion and matter, including your past foibles. There isn't a step-by-step guide you can read or programme you can undergo that will do this work for you. Books, courses, and podcasts may help you understand the complexities of confidence, but they won't tell you how to build it, because your story is too unique to be disciplined and structured according to a ten-step programme. Only you can identify the voices in your head which aren't yours; only you can stop comparing yourself to others; only you can revisit your past and make peace with it; only you can uncover which parts of you are authentic and which parts are for show; and only you can learn how to accept yourself. If you want to be accepted by others for who you are, you need to commit to a life of being authentic and accepting yourself for who you are, flaws and all.

CHAPTER FIFTEEN

THE ART OF GROWING UP

'YOU'VE CHANGED.' IT'S STRANGE HOW SUCH A SMALL and benign statement can feel so painful. When I came back from the army, I heard it all the time, from my friends, siblings, and even my parents. I think hearing it from them stung the most. 'You've changed' is a loaded statement, and it's not usually intended as a positive one. It's usually a coded way of saying 'You're not the person I remember, and I don't like that. You're not what I expect you to be like, and I'm not sure I want to know this version of you.'

People hate change; they hate changing jobs, homes, beliefs, locations, routines, clothes, opinions, and relationships because of the unpredictability of the outcomes. There's always a sense of self embedded in a person's state of being, so when that changes (for either the person or someone who knows that person), there's a discomfort in confronting the unfamiliar. The first time people told me I had 'changed', I started thinking the worst of myself. They sounded so disappointed, almost deflated in who I was. That one small phrase made me feel two inches tall. They made me feel like change was a bad thing, but what I came to realise, through their rejection, was that I wasn't in the wrong for changing. Just because they didn't know who I was anymore didn't mean I'd gone through anything inauthentic or wrong; I just hadn't stayed the same as they had.

The older people get, the more averse to change they become, particularly amongst their peers. Older people become more self-assured in their way of thinking; they believe they have the whole world figured out by their age, and they clog their ears up to anything different, particularly the naive opinions of those younger and less experienced than them. Note, when I say *older people*, I'm referring to adults of any age. Change, you see, is regarded by many as a sign of immaturity. People who jump from fad to fad are regarded by many as immature, along with those who jump from one relationship to another or who change their hair or style frequently. This is a somewhat controversial statement to make (particularly to those of you who do these things and become defensive at the idea of being regarded as immature), but there's logical reasoning behind this association. Frequent and rapid changing is associated with children and teenagers; they jump from friend to friend, toy to toy, favourite cartoon to favourite cartoon, idol to idol, musician to musician. Teenagers are renowned for changing their styles frequently, jumping between career ideas, moving from one fad to another, and chasing every stylish trend that comes along in order to attain popularity amongst their peers. Because teenagers and children are so renowned for changing their identities and interests so frequently, the concept of change, in general, becomes associated with youth and, thus, immaturity.

CHANGE SHOULDN'T BE AVOIDED

This subconscious, negative association between change and

maturity does the concept of change a disservice. The beauty of your childhood and teenage years was the transformation you underwent. You experimented with your sense of self, and even if your motives weren't always pure or in your best interest, you experimented regardless and learned from your mistakes. You learned the hard way about changing to please others or changing to fit in. You learned how it feels to be outcast for what you love and for who you are, and you learned what it is like to fall out of love with things without damaging your sense of self. When you were young, change wasn't such a serious thing; it was a way of living. You changed because it was fun and you weren't so invested in concreting your reputation and image in the world. Nobody expects a six-year-old to be the same person when they're eight, nor would they expect a sixteen-year-old to be the same person when they're eighteen. Unfortunately, this changes when people become adults.

Adults aren't expected to change. People enter relationships in their mid-twenties and expect the person they've married not to change in five years' time. They're shocked when their university buddies are totally different three years after graduation, and parents are horrified to hear when their adult children have changed their ethics, diet, or careers as of last week. Adults aren't expected to change because they're supposed to have it all figured out, from their relationships to their dreams and ambitions. As an adult, you're expected to keep the same friends, stay in the same relationship and career field, and maintain the same hobbies and interests. Whilst there's nothing wrong with living your life the same way for years and years if it fulfils you, it shouldn't be the expected norm.

Change is a wonderful, evolutionary process which you should embrace past childhood. Of course, I'm not promoting that you return to your teenage years and invest in rapid and thoughtless transformations to fit in with the crowd (like job hopping or moving from relationship to relationship because you're bored), but I'm saying you shouldn't shun the idea of change entirely. People shouldn't be so shocked when someone they knew a year ago has changed, nor should they be shocked when they discover that what they want from a relationship in their thirties isn't the same as what they wanted in their twenties. You shouldn't feel ashamed or guilty for wanting different friends in your life than the ones you already have, nor should you feel trapped in a career which no longer appeals to you the way it did a few years ago.

Humans are like trees: they grow under states of crisis. How I grew under my parental care is very different from how I grew during my time in the army, which was also very different from how I grew during my time living in Australia and New Zealand. My change caused a permanent rift in my old relationships: my relationship with my sister broke apart, my father and I stopped talking to each other, and it took years for my mother to finally accept who I was. Losing significant relationships is always upsetting, but rather than allowing myself to wallow in the sadness and cave in to the pressure to revert to who I once was to appease them, I chose instead to accept the loss and work with what I had left. I preferred who I had become, and if I couldn't be accepted for who I wanted to be by people I loved, I would find others who would accept and love me.

Growing up requires you to take responsibility for yourself so that you can take risks and grow from the outcomes, regardless of whether they're good or bad. Personal growth is a phenomenal journey, but it is dependent on you keeping only quality relationships in your life, including the relationship you have with yourself. You may find yourself confronted by the fact that your friend, partner, or even relative isn't the person they were to you a year ago, or perhaps you may not be what you were to them. There's no need to feel insecure or threatened by this difference. All of us should grow in life, but sometimes we don't grow together, and that's OK. Growing apart is healthier than not growing at all.

THE DIFFERENCE BETWEEN MATURITY AND IMMATURITY

What I learned through my personal experience was that the people who I thought I needed in life weren't who I needed at all. I have coached many people, mainly men, in their late forties and fifties who were still dependent and reliant upon their families, usually their mothers. They would still rely on their mothers to do their chores for them, cook their meals, or dictate their personal lives. Whilst not doing your own laundry or cooking may seem like primitive and stereotypical markers of an immature person, there are more precise and less overtly comical ways of distinguishing a mature person from an immature one. The first is the desire to teach others rather than rely solely on being taught.

Now, don't get me wrong, we should never stop learning in life. You can never learn enough about the world around you, or even enough about yourself, for that matter. However, mature people combine their desire to learn with their desire to spread knowledge. Mature people dedicate their lives to investing not only in education but also in other people; they share what they've experienced, the mistakes they've made, and the lessons they've learned. Immature people tend to hold back; they keep themselves guarded and their knowledge under wraps. Most of them refuse to admit they've ever made mistakes in the first place and keep their private experiences to themselves (unless there's an opportunity to boast).

The second distinction between maturity and immaturity is their propensity for self-criticism rather than self-evaluation. This is where many readers now will shrink back in their seats because, of course, every person with low self-esteem criticises themselves. Being open to criticism is an admirable feature, and being self-aware enough to know one's flaws and proactively seek to minimise them is noteworthy, but there is nothing endearing or beneficial about a self-critical person. A mature person doesn't ignore all their flaws or believe they are immaculate. They never berate themselves for their shortcomings and faults; instead, they evaluate themselves.

Evaluation involves honest feedback without beratement, chastisement, belittling, or shame. Mature people accept that they have only ever done their best with where they were in life: mentally, emotionally, physically, and spiritually. They treat themselves as they would treat their child self, and they would never dream of calling their seven-month-old self a useless, pathetic, and worthless creature because they hadn't learned to walk or talk yet, because they understand their seven-month-old self has limitations. It cannot yet run a marathon or start up a new company because, as a seven-month-old, it can only be expected to do so much with the little life experience and mental capabilities it has.

This sentiment extends to every stage of your past self, whether it was you ten years ago or you just yesterday. Your experience and knowledge are always limited, so there is absolutely no point imposing the standards attributed to hindsight on your past self. You may not be good enough now, but that doesn't mean you never will be. Likewise, you may have failed in the past, but that doesn't mean you would fail if you were to try again today. Mature people reflect on areas for improvement; they take note of what parts of a conversation didn't go well and commit to improving at the next opportunity they get. They don't tear themselves down, die of embarrassment and shame, or punish themselves for their shortcomings. They simply learn and move on by acknowledging their faults but not allowing themselves to be defined by them.

Thirdly, mature people prioritise fulfilment over happiness (a distinction we already discussed in chapter six). Prioritising fulfilment means mature people seek opportunities for growth over those for pleasure. It may sound hard to believe, but there are millions of people in the world who do not want to grow. They're very happy living in bubbles of comfort and routine; they know what foods they like to eat, what kinds of people they want to associate with, and what places they want to visit (or not visit). They're more than happy to live their whole life in the same home, surrounded by the same people, and live the same lifestyle they always have. They don't enjoy thinking, reflecting, or working through their mental health, relationship issues, or life goals. They see little to no use in searching for lessons in life or evaluating circumstances because they believe they have no autonomy in life. Life is just something that happens to them, not something they can transform and change.

GIVING VERSUS GETTING

Immature people see life as a five-year-old child sees a sweet shop: they know what they want from it, and if they get it, they're happy. If they don't, they become miserable. When they don't get what they want, they claim 'life's not fair' and they become downbeat, angry, resentful, and depressed. This is because happiness is primarily associated with **getting**: they are happy when they get good grades, when someone likes their status or Instagram post, when they get given gifts, when a stranger compliments them, or when they get a promotion or pay raise at work.

There are some people who like to stir the pot when it comes to this topic by arguing that getting things in life can result in fulfilment. The most common argument is parenthood. They claim that the day they became a parent (i.e., when they got their child) was the most fulfilling day of their life. However, having a baby isn't what fulfils you (although you may have been raised to believe that it is). There are millions of parents in the world, but very few of those parents are living fulfilled lives. What fulfils a parent is not the act of creating a child, but rather the art of raising one. Graduating from university and getting that piece of paper doesn't fulfil you, but the hard work you put in and the lessons you learn do. Attaining that promotion isn't fulfilling, but earning that promotion is. Getting is nice but, in most cases, meaningless. Sure, there can be meaningful instances such as the birth of a child or graduating from university, but in terms of life impact and growth, even these moments lose their emotional impact.

You don't grow as a person because happy moments happen in life; you only grow as a person when you allow happiness to motivate you to become better and develop more meaning. Getting presents, going on holidays, buying a new car, getting those shoes you saved up for, or going to see your favourite singer at a concert doesn't offer lasting fulfilment because the terms of those moments can change. The friend who gave you that awesome present may no longer be in your life two years from now; that singer who you were obsessed with seeing may have been caught up in a worldwide controversy and is now taboo; those shoes you waited months to buy are now worn down, dirty, and out of style three months later.

Happiness is all about getting, and getting is a short-lived experience. Fulfilment, however, is all about **giving**. When you give your resources, encouragement, time, and experience to others, your focus is no longer on yourself; it's on someone else, be that your parent, child, friend, or just some stranger on the street. Think about the last time a stranger turned around and did something for you. How did you feel about yourself and them? What about that friend who gave you some career advice or that colleague at work who helped you during a stressful period? You undoubtedly not only felt gratitude but sheer joy. You may not remember what you got for your birthday last year or how much money someone spent on you, but you'll always remember those times someone made you feel supported, meaningful, and cared for. Likewise, the person who gives to others feels meaningful and worthy because they've extended themselves to another in a way which cannot be bought.

Mature people understand that the world doesn't, and shouldn't, revolve around them. They centre their world around other people and meet other people's needs when and where they can, but with enough self-respect and self-care to accept their limitations. They don't have ulterior motives because the act of giving is a reward enough in itself: it gives their life meaning and purpose. There are so many people out there who have never known what it is like to receive something in life. They've never been given any support, love, or even care, so they waste their lives chasing material things. They want to get everything they possibly can to fill the void within them. They've never received the love, care, or support they've always wanted, so they set themselves on a mission to give themselves everything they possibly can. Unfortunately, not only is this mission meaningless, it's vapid and self-consuming. A person who seeks to get things out of life will only find themselves more isolated and empty.

Mature people see the value in their experiences. They accept and appreciate the story they have to share with the world, and they understand the value they have garnered from their successes, failures, heartbreaks, and joys. Once you start focusing on giving rather than getting, your meaning in life will naturally develop.

CHAPTER SIXTEEN

WHERE ARE YOU GOING?

NOW THAT WE'VE DISCUSSED THE ART OF GROWING UP, the question that remains is: where are you going? As a child, I'm sure you had a vision for your adult self, but unfortunately, making your vision a reality in adulthood can prove to be more confusing and overwhelming than you anticipated. It's easy to picture yourself ageing, leaving home, meeting someone, starting a career, and living alone, but adulthood is never that straightforward. Even if you left home easily, met the love of your life straight away, or found yourself in your dream career with little trial and error, at some point you will have fallen into a state of confusion and wondered, 'Where the hell am I going in life?'

An old mentor of mine once said that if you don't have a significant vision for your life, you'll be forever trapped helping someone else achieve the vision they have for their life. Without personal direction and drive, you'll spend all your energy helping some heartless corporation achieve its financial dreams whilst you slave away for minimum wage without any personal acknowledgment or thanks. Without a vision for your life or having a defined purpose, you'll suffocate in your comfort zone, and you'll never take the risks needed to become your full, authentic self.

But what is a life purpose, and how can anyone possibly know the meaning of their life? It sounds naive and obscene for one man to suggest in his book that he knows the answers to two of the most challenging and profound questions which have mystified centuries of academics, philosophers, scientists, and writers, but I'm not saying I have the answer. No one in the history of the universe is ever going to know the meaning of life, and contrary to popular belief, your life purpose isn't some predetermined destiny which you are on a quest to discover. The only person who can define and determine the meaning and purpose of your life is you, through self-exploration and trial and error.

MEANING VERSUS PURPOSE

Firstly, let's talk about **meaning**. Whilst most people think of meaning in terms of 'the meaning of life is X', meaning has nothing to do with the future. It is a product of your past. All meaning you have in life derives from your past experiences and your interpretations of them. Therefore, the future has no meaning because it cannot be interpreted. Meaning is a self-determined entity: it is *you* who places meaning on certain aspects of your life, from your relationships to your passions, dreams, successes, failures, heartbreaks, and state of being.

Everything you assign meaning to has a multitude of possible meanings; however, you select the meaning which makes the most sense to you based on your interpretation of your past. For example, say you were raised within a single-parent family. Your father left you and your mother and never returned, and your mother didn't treat you very well. There are several meanings you could assign to this part of your life. It could mean that your father was a horrible person, or it could mean your mother was neglectful and selfish, or it could even mean that you were an unlovable and challenging child. Whilst you may agree with several meanings to particular past experiences, there is always one that will bear more weight in your unconscious and will, thus, ultimately impact not only your behaviours but your purposefulness in life.

On the other hand, your **purpose** relates to your future, including your future fulfilment and happiness: who you are willing to become and what you want to achieve. You can only unravel what your purpose is in life by examining and understanding what your life has meant to you up until this point. It's incredibly important to note here that meaning isn't set in stone. Meaning is susceptible to change, which is why it's potentially dangerous to not review and re-evaluate. The idea that meaning can change disturbs some people; they find the very idea of changeable meaning oxymoronic because changeable meaning seems, arguably, meaningless. How can something be meaningful if it's susceptible to change?

Whilst it may sound sacrilegious to the concept of meaning, changing what the past means to you is what therapy and counselling aim to achieve: it's part of the healing process. People are prone to assigning negative and detrimental meaning to their life experiences, which causes all kinds of mental health issues, from low self-esteem to depression, anxiety, and disordered eating. Trained professionals in the mental health industry are there to guide people through the process of assigning new meanings to their experiences and help them recognise that the meanings they assigned to their lives thus far aren't benefitting them. Transforming the meaning you assign to certain elements of your past, from traumas to failures and hardships, helps you alter the relationship you have with yourself for the better. Why wouldn't you want to change the meaning of your childhood bullying from 'I was bullied, so that means I'm a horrible and unlikeable person' to 'I was bullied at school, so that means the person who was bullying me was going through something at home which was upsetting them and they didn't have the support they needed; it had nothing to do with me and who I was'?

THE PROBLEM WITH LABELLING YOURSELF

Once you've begun to understand and potentially adjust the meanings you've assigned to your life, you can begin to identify your purpose: who you are willing to become and what you want to strive for. Again, it's important to note that having a crystal clear image of who you are willing to become isn't about assigning labels to your identity. Labels not only categorise who you are according to predetermined standards, they also reduce your options and impact to a limited sphere of influence. You can label your life purpose as being a parent, an entrepreneur, a writer, or a spouse, but these labels not only limit you to these areas, they also don't ensure quality. Just because you're a mother doesn't mean you're loving, and just because you're a philanthropist doesn't mean you're a good person.

Think about the times in life when you felt at your lowest, when you were the most lost, lonely, and misunderstood. Who did you need at that time? Did you need someone who committed most of the hours of their life to their work and earning money or who was driven by fame and likes online? Did you need a parent, a philanthropist, a partner, or an entrepreneur? Or did you need someone who was loving, emotionally stable, empathic, and caring: someone who was committed to giving others unconditional acceptance and support and wanted to help people find clarity and direction?

It doesn't matter what roles or labels people ascribe to themselves; what matters are the qualities they carry with them and strive to improve with growth and maturity. A parent isn't effective as a parent if they are unloving and cruel; a philanthropist isn't admirable if they are selfish and self-absorbed; a counsellor isn't competent if they are closed-minded and prejudiced; and a spouse isn't an asset if they are unsupportive and secretive.

I want to be a father in life, but my purpose in life is to be a loving, supportive, and available father because I learned from personal experience that just being a father isn't enough. My purpose in life is to be an honest, authentic, congruent, trustworthy, and generous person, and I intend to carry these parts of myself into all areas of my life, from my career, to my family, and the strangers I meet on the street. I want my character to shine before my labels do. It doesn't matter if I'm a father or a famous entrepreneur, a teacher or a success story. All that matters is character and my commitment to growth. My purpose in life is who I am willing to become: the future me who I am open to challenging limiting beliefs and unhelpful behaviours for.

DEFINING YOUR PURPOSE WITHOUT LABELS

The easiest way to define what your purpose is in life is by first identifying what you have lacked in your life. What you lacked in life will help you identify what you need to become for yourself. You know better than anyone what it is like to go through life without something significant, so your purpose in life should be to become the person you never had when you needed them and be that person for others. You can relate to those who need love, support, acceptance, or understanding, so be what those people need.

Unlike labels, which put you under extreme pressure to constantly prove you fit or adhere to them, your character speaks for itself. Stop focussing on whether or not people perceive you as a good enough environmentalist, parent, businessperson, vegan, lesbian, academic, Muslim, athlete, or drag queen; you don't need to prove yourself to anyone. You are what you are, and that doesn't need justification or explanation. What you should focus on instead are the parts of yourself which you can grow in: your honesty, your reliability, your openness, your care, your lovingness, your acceptance, your patience, and so on. It doesn't matter whether or not people think that you aren't Christian enough or that you're not minimalist enough. They're just labels, and they're all defined differently by every person around the world. You can't match other people's standards when it comes to labels, and even if you could, what would be the purpose of it all besides validation?

TAKING CONTROL OF YOUR FUTURE

Everyone wants to achieve something in life that stands for something; everyone has a desire to make a meaningful impact on the world, but few know what that impact would be, and even fewer realise they already have the potential to do so. So people carry on working in the jobs they hate, hanging out with the friends they have nothing in common with, or maintaining the relationship they outgrew five years ago because they prioritise comfort, security, and familiarity over growth. People are frightened about the future because of its uncertainty; they're frightened to have goals and ambitions because they fear failure and disappointment. Whilst I, of course, encourage people to have aspirations in life, I believe more emphasis should be placed on aspirations of self rather than external aspirations. You may not start your dream career, you may not have the ideal family you dreamed of, your plans to travel the world may fall through, and you may not become a famous actress, athlete, or singer, but none of this means you have no purpose or meaning in life.

Most of your future is uncertain because you can't control external factors; you can't control how people treat you, what happens to your job in six months' time, or even certain health conditions. However, the one thing you can control is yourself. You can control your personal development, which habits you foster, which behaviours you manage, and which thoughts you challenge. You can control your outlook on life, how you approach relationships, and your standards.

Where you're going in life has more to do with your growth than your destination: it's about what you choose to move on from, the thoughts you adopt and those you reject, the lessons you learn, and how you approach the problems you face in life. If you want to rebel against the *status quo* and live a life beyond conformity, you have to stop looking for meaning in life and stop assigning purpose to external factors and circumstances. Rather than allowing yourself to dwell upon how the past has made you feel broken, unloved, and worthless, your new meaning should empower you to adopt a reach which constantly extends your grasp: a reach which strives to give more, be more, and build more in the world around you.

Conquering the self requires an understanding and redefining of the meaning of your past so that your vision for who you are and who you are willing to become is clearer. If your destination in life is one of infinite selfhood and growth, you'll never feel lost or misplaced ever again. The map is within you, not without, and it is you who wields both compass and direction.

CHAPTER SEVENTEEN

LEARNING HOW TO FEED YOUR HUNGER

NOT EVERYONE IS COMFORTABLE WITH THE IDEA OF being a teacher. When I tell my clients and students that sharing their stories and passing on what they've learned in life will make their life more purposeful and fulfilled, a lot of them clam up because their mind immediately goes to teaching. They can't see themselves giving lectures online or speaking in front of a group of students, so the idea of teaching others the lessons they've learned makes them feel insecure and insufficient.

Whilst teaching has given my life purpose, it's not the only method for sharing your skills, insights, understanding, and lessons. You don't have to become an instructor, teacher, or life coach to share your stories with the world. You can write blog posts, articles, create videos on YouTube, produce a podcast, join a community group, become a figurehead in a youth group, or volunteer with an organisation or charity. 'But what on earth could I teach or give advice on?' people ask me. 'I don't know anything. I'm certainly not an expert in anything.'

You may not be an expert in psychology, philosophy, or meditation like everyone else seems to be nowadays, but that's not an issue. When I encourage people to start teaching others in order to improve their own learning abilities, I'm not expecting them to pursue doctorates or pick an interest and read every book in that field. You don't need to be an expert or scholar within a particular field to teach people meaningful and valuable lessons. You just need to know your life. You are already an expert of being yourself; nobody else knows you better than you do, and nobody knows what it's like to have gone through your life circumstances with your upbringing and environment. You don't have to be a guru or know all the information out there to help someone broaden or change their perspective for the better.

In season fourteen, episode twelve of *The Simpsons*, Marge assures her daughter Lisa that she and Homer will be able to afford her college tuition, despite Homer's low salary. In order to supplement the income and reassure Lisa of her college tuition, Marge announces the following:

Marge to Lisa: But...I could give piano lessons!

Lisa: But you don't play the piano...

Marge: I just gotta stay one lesson ahead of the kid!

As funny and as somewhat ridiculous this small scene is, it's an accurate and effective approach to teaching. You don't need to be an expert of anything to teach something: you just need to be a step or two ahead of your students. Whilst having more experience and extensive familiarity around a subject is useful, you shouldn't hold yourself back from sharing knowledge with others just because someone out there knows more than you do. Imagine you've just started a new job as a barista and you're on a training day with a couple of other new employees. You're all learning how to use the machines and make certain coffees, and you've found out you're really good at steaming milk. However, one of your fellows is really struggling with the steamer and keeps burning the milk. It wouldn't be arrogant or patronising for you to offer to show them how you steam milk; it would be considered a demonstration of camaraderie. The same can be said for your life experience and life lessons in general: you only have to be a step ahead of another person to offer someone value and support.

THE FOUR STAGES OF LEARNING

However, before you can teach, you must become a student of life. This means you must be willing to learn from your mistakes, failures, successes, and pain, and this isn't as straightforward as it seems. Learning is not a habit that can be employed passively. It's a continuous yet still cyclical process that requires conscious effort and dedication. I refer to the learning process as a four-step cycle which starts with **hunger**. Think about the topics you loved as a child, whether dinosaurs, animals, space travel, ancient history, or literature: the topics and subjects you were eager and hungry to know more about. It didn't matter if you had a teacher guiding you through the topic or a parental figure who influenced your interest; you were always hungry to know more about these topics because the hunger came naturally to you. When you grew up, you became jaded and were likely discouraged from exploring topics and aspects of the world that didn't fit your academic curriculum or serve your employment prospects. Thus, as you got older, you conformed and channelled your energy elsewhere and settled for jobs and lifestyles which didn't drive you to dig deeper.

Hunger is the fuel responsible for kickstarting everything you pursue in life, including personal development. Unless you're hungry to learn more about yourself and grow professionally and personally, you're never going to have the patience or drive to read, watch, or listen to podcasts, books, or videos about personal growth and the psychology behind how you are the way you are. It's only once you have the hunger that you start **learning** (step two).

Learning takes all forms, from formal and structured, such as books, lectures, and videos to real-life events, relationships, and experiences. Learning requires a reflective study of not only your own life but the lives of others. The biggest error many people make when applying themselves to learning something new is allowing themselves to stop there because they believe that reading a few books or taking online courses is enough. Learning requires more than just the absorption of knowledge; it requires embodiment.

You've probably met a few know-it-alls in your life: those people who regurgitate information for the sake of showing off. They pride themselves on how much they know about certain topics, and they strive to make sure others know just how much they know about something. Being knowledgeable is admirable, and it can be incredibly useful within certain fields and professions, but knowledge is most useful when it is embodied and applied in life rather than merely regurgitated. Rather than tell people about the lessons you've learned, show them: lead by example and incorporate what you learn into your personal and professional life.

Once you embody the lessons and principles you've learned, you can begin the next stage of learning: **teaching**. Whilst you may feel uncomfortable taking a teaching role in life, teaching others will make you more confident in your approach and understanding of what you teach. Repetition breeds familiarity, meaning the more you share and teach others what you've learned through your mistakes and experiences, the more familiar you become with these lessons and what they mean to you. Teaching opens you up to dialogues with others who challenge, disagree with, or have alternative perspectives to you, which ultimately opens you up to the final stage of learning: receiving **feedback**. The process of learning can become an isolating and biased experience when conducted within the bubble of the self. Feedback reminds you that no one is perfect and that your experiences, perspectives, and learning approaches are limited and subjective based on your background, environment, personal strengths, and weaknesses.

Receiving feedback should then, ultimately, ignite your hunger once again, as it should encourage you to deepen and challenge your understanding of what you thought you knew to strengthen your position on the subject matter. Feedback is crucial for instigating the learning cycle, which is why it's so incredibly dangerous and detrimental for people to hide within closed bubbles and sects of like-minded people, hiding away from opposing voices or battering them down with unkind or vicious words. True learning cannot take place within a bubble, and I encourage all of my readers to not be afraid of listening to all perspectives in order to learn about them, understand the psychology behind them, and strengthen your own position in accordance with them. Many people out there want to preach about their ideas, but very few are willing to continue the process of learning. Nothing screams ignorance more than someone who thinks they know all the answers. Never block your ears from listening to feedback, even if you'd never believe or agree with it. Your growth and wisdom depend on listening to others, hearing what they have to say, and making your own independent judgment based on the information you have at hand.

CHAPTER EIGHTEEN

LEVEL UP YOUR LIFE

WHEN I WAS A CHILD, I WAS OBSESSED WITH *SUPER Mario*. My consoles were the bulky yet timelessly classic Sega Mega Drive and Nintendo. It took me a little while to warm up to *Super Mario*. I found the first few rounds too easy; they were boring and unchallenging. It wasn't long, however, before I finally met the first boss monster, then the next, and the next. That's when the game became interesting. Each boss monster was increasingly difficult and frustrating. As I progressed through the levels, it took me much longer to formulate the strategies needed to defeat them and avoid their attacks. Some levels took me hours or even days to complete because the boss monsters kept throwing me off guard. They became less predictable and more random, and their attacks were more powerful. But all the stress, yelling, and slamming the controller on the floor was worth it, because each time I beat a boss monster, I levelled up.

Real life follows the same pattern. As you grow, you are faced with more challenging and hurtful circumstances and events, which you learn to manage and overcome. You develop and strengthen the skills, strategies, and methods necessary to handle particular challenges further on in life through repetition and perseverance. It may sound ridiculous, but Harry Potter serves as a perfect example of this. When he first faces Voldemort, he's a young, inexperienced wizard. Thankfully, Voldemort in the early stages is weak and underdeveloped, so Harry is capable of defeating him. However, as the years progress, both Harry and Voldemort grow in strength; the challenges Harry faces become much more complex and dangerous, but because he grows in both understanding and skill, he is capable of defeating the Dark Lord at each stage. Furthermore, Harry realised the importance of teaching others what he knew, which is why he established Dumbledore's army and taught all the students within it the rare and ancient Patronus charm. Harry wasn't a qualified teacher, but his unique experiences had given him an insight into magic that nobody else had. Like most of us, Harry didn't particularly want to be a teacher, and he didn't go about thinking of himself as a teacher; he merely recognised the benefit of sharing his knowledge. He realised what he had gone through had taught him life-saving techniques which would benefit not only others but the wizarding world as a whole, so he shared his knowledge with those he could.

Whilst you may not be able to quantify your growth by the effectiveness of your spells or your ability to ward off an evil overlord and his army in a battle at a magical school somewhere in Scotland, your level in life still exists, albeit it's less obvious to take note of your growth. There's a reason why you used to scream hysterically when you fell down at the age of two but now laugh if you trip on the street with all of your friends watching. You've gone through levels of experience and pain that have taught you what you can manage and cope with.

HOW THE FIXED MINDSET PREVENTS YOU FROM LEVELLING UP

People make a mistake in life, an error of judgment, or a failure and feel scarred by the experience; they deem themselves incompetent and refuse to try again. They believe their failure and pain mean they're inherently incapable, so they avoid intimate relationships, trying for a new career, leaving a relationship, going back to school, or starting a business. The older they become, the more they stop believing in their ability to grow. They don't believe they can learn new strategies or gain new skills, be they professional or personal. They stop believing they can be any other way than how they are today. They genuinely believe they're just underconfident, shy, uncharismatic, unskilled, untalented nobodies, and that's how they'll always be.

If you relate to any of this, it's time to recognise how you're holding yourself back from levelling up. Just because you cannot do something or be a certain way right now doesn't mean you never can be. There will be times in life when you can't do something or you don't cope well with something, but these cases do not reflect your ability. They merely reflect the level you are at in life. Think about all the cringe-worthy, humiliating, and stupid things you did in your teenage years, from the ridiculous lies that you told to the drama you stirred up, the unhealthy relationships you fostered, the mistakes you made, and the mundane things you passionately invested yourself into. When you look back at your younger self, you probably often find yourself cringing and wishing you could go back in time and apply the wisdom you have now to your past self. However, had you known back then what you know now, you would never have learned the information you know today. You had to make those mistakes to be in a position of wisdom. Were it not for your foolish younger self, you'd never have grown into the person you are today, so it's important to keep that in mind and thank your past self for all the ridiculous and embarrassing shenanigans.

THE GAME WON'T LOWER ITS DIFFICULTY TO MATCH YOUR NEEDS

Levelling up is a much more palatable and less offensive way of reminding yourself that ageing doesn't automatically remove you from the realm of immaturity and naivety. Look at how much you've changed since your teenage years. You grew up from that person you once were because your teenage self didn't invest so heavily in the idea of stagnation. Teenagers accept that they need to grow up; actually, they can't wait to grow up. Once you become an adult, however, you're less willing to grow up (let's face it, none of us like the idea of ageing). The moment you were classified as an adult, you most likely believed that who you were became set in stone forever, that you'd reached your peak maturity, and that all character traits you possess in adulthood are the ones you're destined to carry to the grave. The only way you can overcome this prideful adult status is to stop taking yourself so seriously and admit that you still need to grow up a little more, or rather, level up.

A game doesn't lower the level of its boss monsters to match your level of ability. If you haven't gone through the training (either by dodging fights with enemies or cheating your way through), you'll find yourself unable to beat the end-of-level boss and end up stuck on the same level forever. Life is the same: the world won't bend to suit your needs. The world and the systems in it cannot give you special treatment in life just to help you progress whilst remaining in your comfort zone. You can't expect to grow in business without networking, a job won't just land in your lap if you don't put yourself out there, and you'll never develop meaningful relationships if you avoid all emotional situations because they make you feel uncomfortable. I'm not saying you need to change yourself to please other people, nor am I saying that introverts should force themselves to become extroverts or that less emotional people should be ashamed of themselves. What I am saying, however, is that you cannot expect to get far in life if you remain exactly the same, fixed within the realm of your comfort zone. Always be authentic to yourself, never feel ashamed or inferior because of who you are, but understand that you need to be lenient at times and push yourself out of your comfort zone in order to get ahead in life.

You can't be offended that no one comes up to you at networking opportunities if you spend the whole evening glued to the wall without cracking a smile or making any eye contact because 'I'm a shy, quiet introvert and that's just the way I've always been'. The environment and society within it are not going to adapt to suit your preferences; you're either going to have to work with the strengths you have or accept that you cannot be part of certain environments because you're unwilling to be part of them. If you refuse to adapt your attitudes, behaviours, and personality traits to fit within your ever-changing environment, you'll find yourself stuck on the same level throughout your entire life.

TALENT ISN'T ENOUGH

One overlooked but hugely important aspect of levelling up in life is motive. People jump into the deep end and start looking for easy, three-step guides for 'how to do the things you're passionate about in life' or start taking quizzes online to give them some starting point and direction. I can tell you categorically that there isn't a single quiz or guidebook in the world that will tell you what your motives are. Only you know why you do what you do and what you genuinely want out of life.

The reason you feel so lost and confused is that you've been unable to pinpoint and identify your motives in life, thanks to society's emphasis on talent. In a world completely governed and driven by the narrative of talent, your motives are completely undermined by your sense of inferiority. Most of your ambitions, drives, and motives in life are slashed immediately upon contemplation because you've been conditioned to determine and evaluate whether or not you are gifted, talented, attractive, or smart enough to pursue the things you want to in life. So many people never attempt to level up because they believe they lack the talent to do so; they believe they're inherently limited and inferior and thus remain as they are within their bubble. However, what most people fail to realise is that talent doesn't get them anywhere unless it is applied alongside hard work.

Imagine a world in which talents could be given out like sweets at Halloween. In this world, the CEO of a company decides he wants to take a vacation, so he picks two of his favourite employees to manage aspects of the company in his six-month leave. He gives ten of his personal talents to each of the employees and says they can do whatever they'd like with them for the benefit of the company. Six months later, the CEO returns, excited to see what his employees have done with the talents he left them, so he calls each of them into his office one by one. The first employee enters the office with a wheelbarrow full of talents. 'You won't believe it', he cries to his boss excitedly. 'Once I started using the talents you gave me, they started growing by themselves! I've had the most incredible six months. Thank you for loaning me your talents.'

The CEO smiles and congratulates the employee. 'You don't need to thank me; you grew these talents all by yourself with the hard work and time you put into your projects. I'm so proud of you that I believe you've earned every single one of them; I don't want any of my talents back. They're yours to keep and keep on growing.'

He then sends for the second employee, who enters carrying only the same ten talents he'd been given six months ago. He tells his boss that he'd been scared about having the talents because he knew how hard his boss worked and he doubted his own ability to use the talents effectively. He explains to his boss that he buried them in his desk rather than using them, and kept them safe for when the boss came back rather than risk using them poorly. Despite having not gained any, he was proud that he hadn't lost any of the talents and that he was returning them in the same condition that he'd been given them.

The CEO is hugely disappointed and, to a degree, quite angry. He had expected progress from his top employees and wanted to see his company prosper in his absence, but was let down by the fear of another. After hearing his employee's excuses, he takes back the talents he had loaned him and sends him back to his desk to continue the work he'd done before, with no interesting projects or tasks to work on and no new talents to show for it.

YOUR MOTHER WAS RIGHT

The mistake the second employee made is the same mistake most people make in life: he put more thought and effort into getting it right than doing his best. Most people respond with exasperation to the idea of doing their best because they've internalised the phrase as the language of losers. You're probably familiar with mothers and naive and peppy teachers telling children to do their best before then squeezing the child in a supposedly comforting tight hug with an exaggerated smile plastered on their face. People think they were only ever told to do their best because others lacked faith in their ability to do well. Doing their best was a cold-comforting reminder that everyone else was better than they were, but it wasn't supposed to matter because Mummy still loved them and was proud regardless.

When you were younger, you didn't want to be coddled and told to do your best: you wanted to get it right. Back then, you couldn't imagine your favourite actors, sports heroes, entrepreneurs, celebrities, and famous inventors being told to do their best by their parents. They didn't need to do their best. They knew how to get it right. Whilst it's less glamorous and exciting to visualise those you admire being told by their grandparents and parents over a bowl of cereal to just do their best, the truth of the matter is, your mother was right. It may have sounded lovey-dovey and patronising when you were younger, but your mother wasn't telling you to do your best because she thought it would help soften the blow when you failed. She was telling you to do your best because it's more efficient and effective than trying to get it right.

As we saw from the CEO story, the employee who was focussed on getting it right took no risks and therefore made no progress professionally or personally. He wanted to avoid being seen as a failure or even as an average employee, so he didn't use the talents he was given and instead buried them away for no one to judge and critique. Getting it right focuses more on how you are perceived by others than how you perceive yourself. When you don't want others to see your inexperience and confusion at trying something new, you stick to what you know really well and play it safe. However, when you stick to what you're already good at, you stop trying your best; you take the easy route. There's nothing challenging or character-building about playing the same game at the same level over and over again. Sure, being able to sail through life flawlessly may look impressive to others in terms of having a clean record, but it does nothing for your growth or the respect others have for you.

People don't want to work with those who are driven to get it right for the sake of egocentric self-preservation. They want to work with people who want to be their best and do their best for both themselves and the organisation and society they are part of. They don't care if people take risks (provided they're not reckless), nor do they mind when people fall flat on their face and make mistakes. People are interested in those who are more committed to striving for their best than those playing it safe, limiting their energy, and not pushing the boat out.

Levelling up isn't about getting things right. There is no right way to beat a *Super Mario* boss monster. You either beat it or you don't. You can either give up and leave the game on the same level, or you can keep trying and keep progressing through the game. Some people will beat the boss monster more quickly than you do, and others may use a different technique to beat the boss monster, but none of that matters.

Take inspiration from how others level up in life, learn from their mistakes and successes, but never compare yourself to them. Use what you learn from the examples around you to inspire the best in yourself. You'll find that you'll become more productive and effective in life when you stop trying to get it right and just start giving your best.

CHAPTER NINETEEN

DEVELOPING EMOTIONAL INTELLIGENCE

IN A WORLD WHICH OVER-GLORIFIES ACADEMIA AND IQ levels, the lack of emotional-intelligence education is painfully staggering. We live in societies where bad and unhealthy relationships between families, lovers, friends, and strangers are commonplace and are often accepted as the norm by those within them. Unhealthy relationships are plastered all over tabloid websites, YouTube, and daytime television, and millions of people around the world are seeking therapeutic and medical help for the mental issues caused by their past relationships and inability to feel emotionally stable. Emotional intelligence is about understanding your emotions and responding to them effectively to produce an outcome that you want. Having the ability to understand and respond appropriately to your own emotions also enables you to better understand and perceive emotional responses from others and, in turn, respond to others in an emotionally appropriate manner.

When people start committing to personal development

and pursuing their goals in life, it's easy for them to forget about training their emotional responses. They concentrate so much on working through their negative thought processes, identifying their values, and working through their self-worth issues that they often critically overlook managing their emotions. Imagine this scenario: a person is going all out for a promotion at work, putting in all hours of the day and showing their boss their dedication, time management skills, and talent, but then all of a sudden, someone else gets the job they wanted. Then what? That person breaks down; they become infuriated, disappointed, and heartbroken. They may cry, scream at their partner, and binge on food which isn't the healthiest, ultimately leading them down another spiral of unhelpful emotions.

Emotional intelligence isn't about removing anger and sadness from the equation. It's about managing your emotions to produce more effective results. Anger and sadness are completely valid, but they can either motivate you to quit and give up or they can motivate you to strive even harder than before and energise your determination.

HOW TO DEVELOP EMOTIONAL INTELLIGENCE

Emotional intelligence theories have been divided into three distinct models: the Ability Model, the Mixed Model, and the Trait Model. The model I've found the most effective is the Mixed Model, which was coined by science journalist Daniel Goleman. Goleman approached emotional intelligence in terms of leadership performance and argued that it could be presented as an array of personal management skills: self-awareness, self-regulation, social skills, empathy, and motivation. The Mixed Model proposes that emotional intelligence is critical for success, healthy interpersonal relationships, managing conflict, and adapting to changing environments. The question is, how do you develop emotional intelligence? Like any skill in life, emotional intelligence is something you need to learn, practise, and develop over time.

REFLECT ON YOUR OWN EMOTIONS

When people read that they should reflect on their emotions, their minds immediately go to meditation. Meditation is a fantastic tool, which trains people to not only regulate and manage their emotions but also to identify and categorise their thoughts and feelings. However, many people make the fatal error of reserving reflective thought for meditation sessions only, and they fail to engage in reflective thought throughout the rest of their day. This means that even a dedicated meditation-lover would only reflect upon their emotions once a day, which, I'm afraid to tell you, isn't nearly enough. You need to reflect on your emotions regularly throughout the day in order to make emotional management a habit. The best way to do this is within the few moments after you have an emotional response to something, such as when your boss tells you off at work, when your friend becomes more distant from you, or when there's a long queue at a supermarket and you're starving, tired, and just want to go home.

Taking the time to reflect upon your own emotional responses to particular incidents throughout the day will not only make you more mindful of what elicits particular emotional responses, but you'll also become aware of the emotional patterns of the responses you produce, which you can trace back through your history and unfold in your spare time to help you understand yourself better.

OPEN YOUR MIND TO NEW PERSPECTIVES AND UNLOCK YOUR EMPATHY

Once you've begun to understand your own emotions, you can start extending your emotional understanding to help others feel understood. You may not always judge someone's emotions correctly, but just theorising about them can help you adjust and manage your emotional responses in a way that would benefit you. For example, say your boss is telling you off for incredibly unjust reasons. It would be easy for you to become upset or angry and potentially either spend your day or month in misery, internalising all the blame he assigned to you, or respond in anger and say something in an unprofessional manner to your boss that results in you getting fired.

Taking your boss's emotions into consideration, even on a hypothetical level, can break you from responding with a knee-jerk reaction. Perhaps they're stressed at home because their spouse is sick or they've had a new baby. Maybe their anger toward you is the only way they can manage their disappointment in you, or perhaps they're grieving for the loss of their mother and they don't have anyone to talk to, so their emotional outlets target their employees. None of these things may be true, and none of these things excuses your boss of mistreating you at work, but taking a moment to evaluate the other person's potential emotions and reasoning behind their emotions protects you from making unwise emotional moves. You don't want to live a life of internalised shame or uncalculated and immature anger; you want to be a master of your emotions. Practising empathy and opening yourself up to viewing circumstances from alternative perspectives (even if they are perhaps based on hypothetical circumstances) will help you make more rational and wise decisions which aren't emotionally lead.

START PAUSING

I'm sure you were warned as a child to think before you speak. The lack of life experience and naivety of children means they tend to say pretty thoughtless and unkind things, even if they're being honest by saying things like 'you stink' or 'she's gotten fatter since we last saw her'. When you were younger, you were likely told to handle certain ideas and opinions with diplomacy and consideration by pausing before you spoke, reflect upon how your message would be received, and determine whether or not your message would inflict unnecessary pain or positive reflection.

However, many people find biting their tongue extremely difficult when they're in emotional situations, and even fewer are capable of calmly responding internally. The second someone receives an email insinuating they've done something wrong at work, they become anxious and frightened. When a friend texts back with a blunt, short reply, they begin to worry that they've ruined the friendship. Or when a driver cuts them off on the motorway, they become immediately furious and filled with hatred for them.

Pausing, even for just a split second, after something happens to you stops you from making reckless and impulsive decisions like emailing your resignation letter to your boss, deleting your friend's number from your phone, or tailgating the driver who cut you off. Being able to pause during stressful and upsetting situations is a challenging process that requires practice, but it'll become easier with time. The next time you feel driven to say or do something out of an emotional response, stop yourself and observe the emotion before taking ten deep, long breaths. If possible, take a walk as well and ask yourself questions such as 'What am I feeling and why do I feel this way?' or

'What are the possible reasons the person acted the way they did?' 'What circumstances may that other person be dealing with right now?' and 'What are the negative consequences of my words and actions?'

IDENTIFY YOUR STRESSORS

Stress is the body's response to the demands of the world, and everyone has different trigger points. Some people are stressed out by children screaming, whilst others are stressed by piles of paper on their desk or bills wiping their bank account clean every month. Effective emotional intelligence requires that you identify the sources of your stress and discomfort and learn how to manage your emotions surrounding these particular aspects of your life. It's not about avoiding your stressors entirely, because no one can expect to lead a stress-free life, but rather learning how to manage your stress and training yourself to become more prepared and equipped for dealing with your stressors when you encounter them.

BECOME MINDFUL OF YOUR VOCABULARY

Being a strong communicator is an essential element of emotional intelligence. There's nothing admirable or mature about someone who can keep their cool during stressful situations but refuses to communicate in any shape or form about how they feel to others. Keeping emotionally steady but remaining totally silent is evasive, dishonest, and unproductive. Being able to articulate your feelings to other people (rather than demonstrating your feelings to them) not only helps maintain a steady emotional environment for mature discussion, but also protects you from stewing in your own thoughts and feelings and allows for others to experience you more authentically.

STOP TAKING OFFENCE AND LEARN FROM CRITICISM

Just because your partner offers you fair criticism every once in a while doesn't mean they don't love you, and just because your boss gives you quite harsh criticism doesn't mean you need to quit your job. Criticism from anyone can be hard to swallow, whether it's on the internet, from your best friend, or from your mother, but not all criticism is ill-intentioned.

It's tempting to label all kinds of criticism as hypocrisy, hate, jealousy, ignorance, or just plain spite, but there is always some elemental truth to the criticism you receive. This isn't to say that all criticism you receive is accurate, but all criticism stems from somewhere rooted in reality. People formulate both accurate and inaccurate criticisms against you through their perceptions of you, which means all external criticism should be followed by self-reflection, particularly on how you present yourself to certain people.

No matter how wildly inaccurate you may believe the criticism to be, discarding all criticism and taking offence is fatally ignorant and unproductive. All feedback you receive is an opportunity to self-reflect and learn about yourself. You can also learn a lot from your critics, such as how you are perceived by others, how your behaviours and emotions unintentionally come across, and (potentially) how to effectively and ineffectively critique other people.

The healthiest approach to negative criticism is to put your personal feelings aside and be grateful for the insight into an alternative perspective, no matter how painful or upsetting that may be. Never focus on how the criticism was delivered, but focus instead on what you can take away from the criticism without becoming emotionally and personally attached to the criticism.

REMAIN PROACTIVE, NOT REACTIVE, EVEN DURING TIMES OF ADVERSITY

Sometimes you will face circumstances that are capable of triggering a complete meltdown: your health takes a turn, you lose someone, your finances are placed in jeopardy, or you are suddenly faced with unemployment and job insecurity. It's incredibly difficult to channel positive thinking during upsetting and frightening times, but the only beneficial response is to acknowledge your emotions, allow yourself to feel them, and then move on. Don't wallow in the feeling, and don't allow your mind to become consumed with helpless and destructive thoughts. Don't complain and throw a pity party for days, weeks, and potentially years after the situation occurs. Focus entirely on asking yourself constructive questions and working your way through and out of your situation.

Don't allow it to take up so much space in your head that it begins to become part of your identity. Don't allow adversity to become part of who you are, and don't become fond of it. Regard adversity as a challenge which you are glad to accept and overcome rather than a sign the universe has thrown your way to stop you moving forward. The universe doesn't care about you enough to throw you any signs. The universe has bigger things to create and focus on than wasting its time trying to ruin your life for the fun of it.

Emotional intelligence is, unfortunately, lacking in this world, and as you grow and develop yours, you will encounter many people who lack it. In these circumstances, it's tempting to stoop down and meet others where they're at, but it's important to uphold your emotional intelligence standards at all times and lead others by example and wish the best for them. Emotional intelligence is a delicate balance of rational thinking, emotional awareness, and expression which requires continuous effort, practice, and focus. It not only allows you to become a better communicator, but it helps you improve your mental well-being, your self-regulation, and your personal and professional relationship management. Once you start managing your emotional intelligence, you will find that others will regard you as more trusting, reliable, and inspirational.

CHAPTER TWENTY

THE SECRET TO OPTIMAL PERFORMANCE

ENTHUSIASM IS INFECTIOUS. MOST PEOPLE ARE EASY to enthuse when it comes to matters of personal betterment. People love to imagine their future selves as a healthy, fit person with an incredibly well-paid, skilled job with ample time to spare in their calendar to travel the world and become world-famous in a hobby they enjoy, all whilst being surrounded by kind and inspirational people. Enthusiasm is contagious. Commitment, sadly, is not.

In 2002, a clinical psychology study conducted by three psychologists looked into the personal progress of two groups of people who were interested in making personal changes. The first group was classified as New Year's resolvers; they committed to making changes at the beginning of the year. The second group made no New Year's resolutions but were still interested in pursuing positive personal growth. The individuals in the groups didn't differ in terms of problematic histories, demographic characteristics, or behavioural goals. What the psychologists found over the next six months was that the resolvers reported back with a higher rate of success than the non-resolvers, with 46 percent of resolvers claiming success, compared to just 4 percent of non-resolvers. The psychologists determined that the resolvers employed more cognitive-behavioural processes but fewer awareness-generating and emotion-enhancing processes than non-successful resolvers.[1]

Most people know what they want to change about themselves, whether it's their confidence, self-esteem, weight, fear of public speaking, introversion, or hyperactivity, but very few actually take the necessary steps for change. People don't take personal change as seriously as they would writing an essay or building a business because they consider it easier. However, personal change is just as complex and detailed as any business blueprint or essay structure. It requires a well-formulated strategy which is broken down into achievable and quantifiable steps.

Change only ever occurs when the desire to change outweighs the desire to stay the same. Taking the easy way is always more tempting for people, and because most don't know how to strategise implementing change, they give up in the early stages. However, all you need is a strategy that supports and maintains your enthusiasm.

HOW TO MAINTAIN YOUR ENTHUSIASM FOR CHANGE

STEP ONE: MAKE THE DECISION TO CHANGE

People often go through life completely oblivious to their

---

1   J. C. Norcross, M. S. Mrykalo, and M.D. Blagys, 'Auld Lang Syne: Success Predictors, Change Processes, and Self-Reported Outcomes of New Year's Resolvers and Nonresolvers', *Journal of Clinical Psychology* 58, no. 4 (2002): 397–405.

thoughts and actions; they never consider that every decision they make in a day shapes their current reality and who they are. If you're unhappy with the results you're currently getting in life, the first things you need to confront are the conscious and unconscious decisions you're making, which are determining who you are and where your life is going. Here are a few ways you can go about making life-changing decisions:

Realise the Power of Decision-Making

Before you make any decision, you need to understand the impact it may have. Any decision you make triggers a consequential chain of events, so it's important to accept responsibility for the consequences that follow. In realising the power of decision-making, you'll gain more clarity and become more successful in making wise decisions and predicting the future. If you're aware of the consequences that might arise, you are more likely to make healthy decisions that support your goals.

Follow Your Gut Instinct

After spending a long time carefully planning, analysing, and considering the pros and cons of a situation before reaching a decision, people become mentally exhausted and usually fall into a state of procrastination. Procrastination gives people the time and space necessary to start doubting themselves, meaning that during this period, they usually become frightened of making any changes. This is why you need to believe in yourself more and learn to trust your gut instinct. Even if you end up making a poor decision, going with your gut will help you become a more confident decision-maker and form a healthier relationship with failure.

Follow Through with Your Decisions

Once you've made a decision, it's tempting to hold off from acting on it until you have collected a few secondary opinions. Whilst it's more than reasonable to give your mother a phone call, call your colleagues in for a meeting, conduct a poll online, or ask your partner for their thoughts, it's easy to get stuck in a state of inaction. There's nothing meaningful or significant about a decision that is never followed through to completion. Ask for some secondary opinions and definitely run your decisions past those who they may affect, but don't procrastinate acting upon your decision by suddenly deciding to conduct a month's worth of market research.

Whilst seeking secondary opinions on your decisions is both sensible and respectful, seeking secondary opinions (or even seeking out too many secondary opinions) on your personal projects can prove fatal. Contrary to your logic (which is probably rooted in the idea that if you share your ideas with others, others will hold you accountable), sharing your goals robs you of motivation. According to a 2009 study conducted by Peter Gollwitzer of NYU, the very act of sharing your dreams, ideas, and goals with others incites premature praise from those around you, meaning you're less likely to follow through on your decisions because your brain has already received the reward it wanted (external validation). This buzz of external validation reads like a success in your brain, which means your desire to achieve something is falsely fulfilled and you then have no desire to actually follow through.

Decisions are pointless if they remain fantasies. It's fun to daydream about applying for that job, changing your style, taking up a new hobby, or starting that online business, but real change in life requires action, the adoption of new habits, and perseverance. I've known people who came up with multimillion-dollar ideas but never followed through with their visions. How do I know they were multimillion-dollar ideas? Because that's what someone else earned from them when they followed through. If you don't claim that domain name, someone else will. If you don't look for funding for that product, someone else will. If you don't write that book, someone else will.

Maintain a Flexible Approach

This may sound counter-intuitive, but making a decision doesn't mean that you shouldn't be open to other options. For example, say you set yourself a goal of losing one stone over the next few months through cardio, but after the first six weeks, you discover that you absolutely hate running on a treadmill and you hate the gym in general; that's totally valid. Rather than cancelling your gym membership and giving up the weight-loss process entirely, a flexible approach would look at all options there are. A flexible person would ask if the gym had a swimming pool or interesting classes they could join; or they may look into exercise classes outside of the gym, such as dance, rock climbing, walking groups, or aerial. Just because someone accomplished the same goal you're after using one method doesn't mean it's the right method for you, so expand your horizons and be open and willing to change your approach when it stops working for you.

Learn from Your Past Decisions

No matter how careful and thoughtful you are, you will have made bad decisions in your life which serve as an excellent platform to base your future decision-making upon. Whilst it's important not to dwell on the mistakes you've made in the past, reflecting on them without shame and chastisement can be productive. You need to ask yourself, 'What went wrong?' 'What can I do differently to make it work?' and 'What did I learn from this?' The truth is that you will mess up at times when it comes to making decisions, but instead of beating yourself up about it, you can choose to learn something from it. In order to avoid any irrational and emotional responses to your analysis of your mistakes, I would recommend writing down your answers rather than keeping them in your head, so they can be approached logically.

Get Excited about Making New Decisions

So many people don't enjoy the decision-making process. Although decision-making might not be the most enjoyable thing in the world, when you practise it more often, it becomes a game of opportunity. Decision-making offers an incredible opportunity to learn more about yourself and become more confident in your convictions and abilities. Embrace the art of decision-making because any decision you make from this point onwards has the potential to affect your life profoundly.

STEP TWO: TAKE ACTION

Everyone wants a rewarding and fulfilling life which consists of good health, positive relationships, a fulfilling career, and having enough money to live comfortably. Unfortunately, most get caught in a mental trap of believing hugely successful people got to where they are in life because of some special gift. You know that rewarding lives don't come effortlessly. Whilst there may be millions of people who climbed up through the ranks thanks to nepotism, there are millions more who earned their way to the top, and those who work hard reap the mental benefits of being at the top over those who were given their status and positions in life.

You need to stop being bitter and disgruntled by those whose lives were given to them on a plate; your hatred of nepotism won't destroy the nepotism, and your sulking won't result in you being blessed with friends in high places who will give you a leg up in life. You need to accept that the world plays out the way it does and that you aren't one of those people, so you're going to have to put in the work and earn it in the most rewarding way possible. The greatest gift that highly effective people have over those who watch the world go by is their ability to take appropriate action.

Some people want to live a life of unlimited prosperity; they want to achieve great things, build successful businesses, travel to interesting places, meet extraordinary people, and have the ability to be as generous as they choose to be. If you want a life like this, you need to take action. Making a decision is always a great start, but taking action is the only practical step needed to start getting results. It may sound obvious, but sometimes the obvious steps are overlooked.

Another issue arises with progression when people rely too heavily on accumulating knowledge rather than putting knowledge into action. They spend years of their life studying particular areas of interest without ever getting their hands dirty, whether that is in finance, art, writing, investing, or life coaching. You could potentially be a world-famous artist, life coach, entrepreneur, writer, or investor, but having the ability doesn't secure success. The formula for achieving results is:

Ability + Strategy + The desire to get a result = Result

The only thing holding people back from acting upon the knowledge and skills they've accumulated is their lack of self-belief. Your belief system is the driving force behind your behaviours and the results you get in life. If you change your beliefs, you will change your behaviours, and when you change your behaviours, you change your results.

There are many things that can keep someone from believing in themselves, from early-life neglect to failure, trauma, and humiliation. However, the reasons behind your low self-belief don't actually matter. You can spend months and years in therapy trying to unpack the psychological source underlying your low self-belief, but the real question you need to ask yourself is: 'Why am I so determined to fail?' Why are you so resistant to changing your lifestyle, beliefs, behaviours, and approaches, even though you know you want to? Why are you so determined to make these ideas not work for you, and why are you determined to find reasons why you won't succeed?

You hold yourself back in life because you prefer playing the victim rather than risk becoming a failure. Successful people don't look for reasons to stay a victim. They are determined to make a situation work out in their favour, so they do whatever they can to make it happen, regardless of how many failures they encounter along the way. The only difference between a successful and an unsuccessful person is their willingness to think about themselves and their situation differently.

BIG RESULTS REQUIRE BIG ACTIONS

A modest idea and an incomplete plan will often produce some form of success when accompanied by appropriate action. Sir Isaac Newton was onto something when he claimed that a 'body at rest tends to remain at rest, and a body in motion tends to remain in motion'. If you do nothing, nothing will happen; if you take minimal action, results will be minimal, and if you take significant action, you will be rewarded with significant results.

Most people find starting the hardest part, mainly because the beginning of a project looks small, insignificant, and trivial. However, the small, insignificant, and trivial matters are responsible for forming the building blocks to greater success and, therefore, must be done. All you need to focus on in the beginning is embracing the approach of starting small. In an age where you are constantly bombarded with digital distractions, being able to start small and work your way up is a huge skill because it requires harnessing the power of focus.

At the beginning of every project (and every day), identify a single task which gives purpose towards your overall goal, and challenge yourself to only focus on it for a reasonable period of time. You can use the Pomodoro technique in this instance, which requires you to work for twenty-five minutes without any distractions, followed by a five-minute break. Twenty-five minutes may not seem like a lot, but if you follow this technique several times a day over a period of several days, possibly weeks, you will instantly increase your chance of success in contrast to your previous state of choosing to do nothing because of fear.

Another effective approach to productivity is to ensure that you spend the first hour of your day working on high-value tasks, that is, those which are most important to your long-term goal. This means avoiding trivial responsibilities such as reading emails and replying to notifications for the first hour of your day at least, as these tasks tend to keep you busy in a way which prevents you from getting any significant and meaningful work done.

Committing to change without a strategy would be like setting out on a car journey to a destination you've never visited before without a map or 'sat nav'. There's a high probability you are going to get lost, tired, and frustrated along the way. However, having a strategy isn't enough within itself. Sure, you can implement a strategy to learn to play piano by watching hours of YouTube videos, but watching seventeen hours of YouTube tutorials won't make you any better a pianist if you never touch a piano. Strategies for personal development are like the blueprints to a house: they're there to guide the construction, but they don't ensure the house is built. Only you can implement your strategies. There's no use having an exercise programme if you don't go to the gym, there's no point in a diet plan if you don't stick to it, and there's no point paying thousands of dollars to attend a training course if you don't do the exercises given or read the required texts before class.

I know you're holding yourself back because you're scared. You're scared of not being as good as you want to be, and you're afraid of not getting the approval and admiration of others. You're afraid that you're not going to make everyone happy all of the time, and you're afraid of disappointing people. All of your fears are valid. In the beginning, you're not going to be as good at something as you'd hoped you'd be, because skills take time to develop, and you're not going to receive approval and admiration from some people because there are people who love to tear others down and resent others for trying to better themselves. You will never make everyone happy, and you will disappoint people from time to time. That's life. You can't keep being afraid of life. You can't hide away and put your dreams on hold because life won't play out in this unrealistic, idealistic way. Accept that you will not please everyone, embrace your imperfections, and prepare yourself to cause some waves. It's time to show the world what you're made of and find out what you're truly capable of.

STEP THREE: MANAGE YOUR STATE

Your physical and mental states play critical roles in your successes and failures. If you are in a state of negativity or defeat, you set yourself up for failure. However, if you place yourself in a positive and productive state of mind, you strategically position yourself in an empowering frame of mind that automatically increases your chance of success.

Your state is determined by three areas of your life. The first is your **physical response to your circumstances**, including what you do with your body and how you produce relevant emotions and feelings. If you approach a task with an energetic and convincing manner, you will have the impetus to carry on and succeed, but if you approach it with an exhausted, depressed, and low physical state, you will be more inclined to give up.

The second area is your **focus**. Your energy in life follows your focus, which means if you spend your life focus on your failures, the negatives, mindless social media, or binge-watching television, your energy will correspond accordingly. Focus doesn't guide action; action guides focus. Think of focus in terms of a camera: you point your camera towards the object or person you want to take a photo of before adjusting the focus to suit the image. This means that there's absolutely no use excusing your decision to spend all weekend watching Netflix with the notion that you can't focus on your project if your focus is on the television or laptop screen. You have to start working on what you want to build focus on before focus can develop.

Your focus is heavily reliant on your ability to choose what you focus on in life, whether that's negative or positive thoughts, television screens or books, social media, or Word documents. You have to eliminate what isn't worthy of your focus, prioritise that which is, and defend the things worthy of focus from all the distractions and lapses in judgment you are prone to. Focus is a skill you need to develop and maintain over a period of time, and in this digitally excitable society, it doesn't come easily. However, if you first work on managing where your internal focus goes (i.e., on positive thoughts rather than negative), external focus issues will become much easier to manage.

The third and final area is the **language you use**, internally and externally. You create meaning out of the questions you ask yourself. The repetition of those meanings creates beliefs. This means that the more you question whether you're good enough, talented enough, lovable, intelligent, friendly, or significant, the more you'll doubt yourself and start deriving meanings from your doubt, which implies you aren't enough in anything in life. However, if you start asking yourself positive and empowering questions, you'll produce dramatically different results compared to asking disempowering and negative questions.

Imagine what your life would be like if you started asking

yourself 'What do I love about myself?' instead of 'Why am I such a loser?' or 'What motivates me to do my very best?' rather than 'Why am I so lazy and unmotivated all of the time?' Getting into the habit of replacing disempowering questions with empowering questions, regardless of your circumstance, will force your mind to direct itself into a positive state. With enough practice and dedication, a positive mindset will become your default state, rather than the negative state you're currently accustomed to.

STEP 4: DITCH THE STORIES

Shame and embarrassment cause most people to make excuses for their failings in life. They claim that they didn't have enough time or money or that they didn't have enough support or the correct information. The more you tell yourself these kinds of stories, the more you will grow to believe them and become comfortable with them. Their reality becomes a convenient and comforting alternative to painful and embarrassing reminders of your failure, so you allow yourself to be held back by them and, in fact, willing to lay on more excuses and stories in order to shelter yourself from the upsetting truth of your past.

If you were, however, brave enough to stop, reflect, and break down the stories you tell yourself (and others) about your failures, you would see a pattern of avoidance and immaturity. You would identify the exaggerations, lies, and blame tactics you employ when avoiding taking responsibility for your failures and shortcomings and see where your attitude (and behaviours) need to change. For example, it may be true you didn't have enough money to do something in life, but that factor doesn't prevent you from saving for it or pursuing it at a later time in life. It may be true that you come from a poor background and didn't have the networking and educational opportunities those from wealthier backgrounds have, but that doesn't excuse you from not trying to network, not attending an educational programme, not reading books from the library, or not taking an online course. The physical and circumstantial limitations you have in life are secondary to the limitations you impose upon yourself through your attitude and beliefs. Some things can never change, but your attitude and beliefs aren't set in stone. Anything achievable in life provides you with the opportunity to take responsibility and ownership of your thoughts and change the ones which are holding you back.

As simple as it sounds, thought-monitoring is a complex skill that requires commitment and self-control. Everything you think, every attitude you adopt, every position you assume, and every perspective you take impacts your thought processes, meaning that you need to monitor them with parental levels of supervision and critique. This isn't to say that you should translate every negative thought into a happy-go-lucky, positive mantra, more that you should evaluate what thoughts and attitudes are holding you back in life and adopt new approaches to them. For example, you can feel shame and embarrassment about certain failures in life. Those feelings are valid, but what you need to change is how you relate those emotions and thoughts to your self-worth. You need to stop being a victim of circumstance and accept responsibility for your failures whilst also forgiving yourself for your limitations. You should assure yourself that you can do better, that you are capable of more, and that you are worthy of success, and remind yourself that your failures don't reflect your future capabilities; they merely reflect what level of life you were at.

Once you start taking stock of the stories you tell yourself, you can begin to analyse why you tell yourself these things and why you fall into the same unhelpful thinking patterns. Start coming up with alternative outlooks and thoughts to adopt, such as, '*I failed and let people down, but I am still worthy of love and respect and I am more than capable of being better than this and I will be better than this in the future*' to replace thoughts such as, '*I failed and let everyone down. I'm such a worthless human being who doesn't deserve to be here and doesn't deserve love or friendship.*'

Mental decluttering is as important as, if not more important than, physical decluttering of your home. Throughout life, you unconsciously adopt depressing, negative attitudes and thinking patterns which trip you up into cycles of negativity and procrastination. Mental decluttering means taking stock of the thoughts, emotional trash, and beliefs holding you back and replacing them with alternative thoughts which align with your desired future self. It's much easier to be productive when you are not weighed down by bags of negativity. The moment you ditch your junk thinking, you will begin to feel lighter and more confident about moving towards the future you want.

STEP 5: GIVE SOMETHING BACK

Everyone has those days where everything seems to go wrong: they get a speeding ticket, the dishwasher stops working, or their zip splits when they're running late. Sometimes what goes wrong is even bigger and more complicated: their best friend moves away, they're suddenly made redundant, or someone they love gets diagnosed with a terminal illness. These more challenging times often leave people wondering what life is really all about and what they are living for.

One of the best ways to cope with life's ups and downs is to be secure in the value you contribute to the world and society. Everyone has the ability to make a significant difference and contribute towards a better world, but not everyone knows what difference they would like to make. However, if they were to start building and working towards a bigger picture in which their contribution to the world extended beyond their own needs and desires, the hiccups of everyday life would become less soul-destroying and unbearable to face.

Framing your life in a way which prioritises making the world better for other people recontextualises how you value yourself in the world. Your focus stops being about how skinny, rich, minimalist, or famous you are and becomes more about how effective and efficient your contributions are to your family, friends, and neighbours. If you're new to the idea of assessing your value and self-worth, identifying how you contribute to others in society may be difficult at first, but every act of kindness you engage in, no matter how small or insignificant it may seem, will inspire others to do the same. Perhaps you're the one who offers a lift to the person whose car is in the garage or the person who takes fifteen minutes out of your day to have a conversation with someone sleeping rough on the streets. There are countless ways to contribute to others and the world, from volunteering to small acts of kindness between strangers.

If you are not sure what you can contribute to the world, consider activities that you're passionate about and ask whether or not they make a positive difference to others in some way and, if not, consider how they can. Ask your friends who know you well to discover what they see as your primary contribution. Be careful not to minimise your contribution; everyone has differing amounts of time and money to give, but all contributions are valuable and everyone has a way of contributing, so do not allow your seemingly 'minimal' capabilities to hold you back from contributing at all. Give what you can to the world and strive to give more when you can, whether that's through having a conversation with that lonely, elderly neighbour who lives in your building or giving someone on the street some food and some company. You have something to give, and sometimes it's the smallest gifts which make the biggest impact.

CHAPTER TWENTY-ONE

PROCRASTINATION: THE ENEMY FROM WITHIN

PROCRASTINATION IS A HUGE PROBLEM FOR MANY people. Over the years, I've heard nothing but reels of perpetual complaints about how people procrastinate even though they don't want to; but for some magical reason, they cannot stop procrastinating. It's as though the world is against them and procrastination is an illness or curse, which has struck them and zapped them of all energy, drive, and motivation. They swear that their procrastination is an inescapable impulse which they're inherently wired to enact against their will. '*I'm a procrastinator, even though I don't want to be*', they say, as though procrastination were part of their genetic makeup like their eye colour or height. 'N*o matter how much I try and force myself to work, I always become distracted.*'

Distraction is almost inevitable in today's world. The majority of people have access to an infinite amount of immediately available information, and it's dangerously addictive. A breaking news story gets uploaded for you to read every fifteen minutes, your friends and family are perpetually posting intriguing statuses detailing their personal lives, and there's always an alluring email popping up in your inbox. Procrastination is easy to rationalise, which is why you so readily engage in it as soon as possible. You seemingly lack the willpower to wait until later to look something up. You could be sitting at your desk, deep in work, when all of a sudden, you wonder what the weather will be this weekend, and rather than just waiting until after work to check up on it, you turn to your phone and open the app.

Humans are inherently driven to want to know about things as soon as possible, yet most of the time, knowing something immediately has absolutely no effect on the actual outcome. For example, after a job interview, you're probably instantly curious about whether or not you've got the job. Waiting for the result of your interview feels like slow torture, but finding out sooner rather than later has no direct impact on the inevitable outcome. The same can be said for social media posts. You're probably guilty of posting a picture on Instagram and immediately refreshing the page to see if anyone has liked it within seconds, and you're likely to repeat checking up on your picture several times throughout the following hour to see if the numbers have gone up.

This immediate desire to know information is scientifically referred to as 'information-seeking behaviour'. From an evolutionary standpoint, humans have developed information-seeking behaviour because their dopamine neurons register information as a reward. This is because knowing where food and water were located allowed their ancestralselves to make better decisions and increase their chances of survival. This is why so many people waste hours of their day scouring the internet for useless information, such as whether the dull itch they have in their left leg is a symptom of a deadly illness. In fact, people spend their whole lives pushing aside all meaningful work related to their more complex initiatives in favour of busying themselves with easy, unimpactful tasks such as checking emails or hashtagging their pictures to hit the Instagram algorithm most effectively.

EMBRACING PROCRASTINATION

The deep irony about procrastination is that whilst it's employed to avoid confronting unpleasant tasks, nobody enjoys procrastinating. Nobody feels proud of themselves or fulfilled at the end of a day of procrastination, yet they continue to engage in it day after day. This is because present bias overvalues immediate rewards and undervalues long-term rewards, and humans fail to accurately rationalise the consequences awaiting them in the future. Nobody likes to be reminded of their mortality, so they don't think about how little time they have left on this planet. As a result, they go about their day believing they have more time to spare than they do. They tell themselves 'that can wait until tomorrow', 'the diet can start Monday', or 'I'll wait until the kids are grown up before I start a business'. Then, after their lives have trickled by faster than they anticipated, they begin to tell themselves it's too late: they'll never accomplish that goal, they're too old, they're not good enough, and their goal is too unrealistic.

The reason you take the time you have so lightly is that, unlike essays and work projects, your life lacks tangible deadlines and retribution to motivate action. You know that failing to meet a deadline in certain circumstances would result in failure, suspension, or severe discipline, which is why you never let your procrastination gremlins get too far out of hand. You can lie around and slack off at work until you come close to the deadline, and then your anxiety and fear kick in and you manically shift into first gear to ensure you complete your tasks. However, when it comes to your career, health, fitness, relationships, and personal growth, there's no deadline to motivate action, so you get caught in a cycle of unending and self-justified procrastination because 'there's always tomorrow'. Trouble is, there's always tomorrow until tomorrow doesn't come.

Procrastination isn't something to be ashamed of, and it's not something you can rid yourself from as though it were a smoking habit. Contrary to what the personal-development world would have you believe, there's no such thing as procrastinators and non-procrastinators. Procrastination is a part of life experienced by everyone, and the only difference between people is their ability to manage their procrastination urges effectively. You can't escape your fate to procrastinate, which is why you've failed so many times at your attempts to attain these impossible standards of workaholic perfectionism and focus. The only thing you can do is learn the skills needed to minimise procrastination and accept that you are going to procrastinate from time to time, no matter how organised and devoted you are. There is no use in abusing yourself with chastisement and guilt trips. These will only fuel further procrastination, and before you know it, ten years will have gone by and you won't have even started.

You know you are more than capable of getting the job done. You've witnessed firsthand how you can kick yourself into gear when it comes down to the wire. You can muster an incredible amount of energy the night before a major presentation, the weekend before you need to file your taxes, or when you're out on Christmas Eve doing last-minute shopping. You have the ability to revise for that exam, pay your bills, or finish the work project right before it's almost too late, because you honour the deadlines given to you and you're frightened of the consequences for not meeting them. However, when it comes to your own life, you don't have deadlines to honour. The government doesn't send out a warrant for your arrest if you don't start your business venture the year you plan to, and your boss wouldn't fire you for not getting into shape within nine months. Most people are more intimidated by socially constructed consequences than naturally ordained ones such as health, ageing, and time because socially constructed consequences are effective immediately. Socially constructed consequences for procrastination hit people hard. They threaten to take away their income, money, home, or status. Natural consequences, however, sneak up on people slowly over time without them realising it, and because people can't see or even feel the consequences of their procrastination, when it comes to their personal goals and ambitions, they fall into a never-ending cycle of letting themselves off the hook.

STOP BREAKING YOUR PROMISES

The obvious solution to all procrastination, therefore, would be to create your own deadlines in life. No one else is going to set deadlines for you when it comes to your personal goals and ambitions. You need to take responsibility for your life and set a deadline to lose the weight, get your first client, launch your business website, pay the bills, or type a certain number of words every day. Without setting your own deadlines, you will never be able to measure your progress and prevent yourself from getting lost in the seas of seemingly never-ending tomorrows. This solution sounds simple enough, yet many people fail to implement it into their lives, because they've broken so many promises to themselves that they don't trust themselves anymore.

You've probably promised yourself so many times to cut down on your social media usage, be more productive tomorrow, and cut out your emotional snacking, but you never do. You tell yourself you're going to wake up at 6 am from now on, exercise every day, and only eat healthily, but you continue to let yourself down to the point that you lose all faith in your ability to change. After broken promise after broken promise, you begin to ask yourself why you should even bother setting deadlines when you know you'll play fast and loose with them and fail to follow through.

Procrastination is one of the core reasons why you trust yourself so little. When you choose to procrastinate, you break a promise to yourself to show up, be better, and make the effort to progress forward in life. Because you've failed to adhere to your promises so many times, you've stopped expecting anything from yourself, and because you don't have to face any consequences for your broken promises, letting yourself down has become an accepted norm. The only way you can build up the trust you've lost is to stick to the promises you make to yourself from now on.

All promises should be taken seriously, regardless of who you make them to. You would never forgive yourself if you broke as many promises to your friends as you do to yourself, nor could you stand to be around someone who treated their promises to you as flippantly as you do. So, it's time to start setting a standard for all the promises you make, no matter who the promises are made to. No one can completely trust someone who has a lifetime history of letting themselves down. Upholding the mental contracts you make with yourself on a daily basis should serve as a blueprint for the dependability of your word to others.

USING DEADLINES TO YOUR ADVANTAGE

When you make a promise to yourself, you should be confident and clear about what you expect from your promise and hold yourself accountable without being disparaging and oppressive. Don't tell yourself your diet starts Monday if you never bother to set yourself an end date with a goal weight, and don't tell your friends and family you're starting up your own company if you haven't given yourself a timeframe to launch within. Deadlines will help you transform your long-term goals into more manageable and tangible short-term goals which you can plan for, reconfigure, adjust, and monitor the progression of.

Nobody enjoys having deadlines in life; no matter how old you get, deadlines probably always remind you of stressful essay assignments or that horrible boss you had years ago. However, deadlines are what you make of them. They are only unbearable and stressful if you manage them poorly. Deadlines serve as powerful tools to increase focus, productivity, and prioritisation. Controlling the timeframe for when something needs to be completed results in controlling the scope of a project. If you give yourself three months to complete something, it will take three months to complete, but if you only give yourself two weeks to do something, you can bet it will get done in two weeks.

Deadlines make you ruthless with how you manage your time

and energy, and they also help you channel your creativity. The idea that creativity can be driven by deadlines sounds paradoxical to those who believe art cannot be rushed, but true creativity isn't about sitting on your hands waiting for inspiration to come to you like a divine vision. It's about motivation and working continuously until your true creative insight comes to fruition.

USING NEUROPLASTICITY TO OVERCOME BARRIERS

There are many core beliefs which cause people to break promises to themselves and procrastinate, but the most common one is their lack of belief in their ability to change. People are quick to dismiss certain lifestyle changes by laying claim to their apparent genetic makeup. They claim they can't wake up earlier because they are a night owl or they're someone who needs nine to ten hours of sleep; they state they can't go vegetarian or vegan because their body doesn't digest vegetables well enough, or they justify their inability to concentrate in meetings or on work projects because they're a daydreamer. People have an excuse for everything, and whilst their excuses may be rooted in truth, their excuses cannot override the scientific reality of neuroplasticity.

Neuroplasticity refers to the brain's ability to change and optimise your neural networks throughout your lifetime. In brief, every time you learn a new fact or skill, your brain changes. Your brain is somewhat like a circuit board comprised of billions of pathways which become active every time you do, think, feel something. Your habitual behaviours, thoughts, and feelings exist along the paths that are most travelled in your brain. Every time you choose to sleep nine hours, eat the same junk food you've told yourself you'd give up years ago, procrastinate, or light a cigarette, the same pathway in your brain becomes active and this pathway becomes stronger, making it easier and easier for your brain to activate this pathway each time it's triggered. This also means it becomes harder to deactivate. This is why addictions, depression, procrastination, and other mental illnesses flourish. Your brain activates the same neurological pathways until they become an automatic response, such as drinking or binge-eating, rumination, or becoming suddenly anxious in crowds or depressed over a certain thought or event. The brain, like people, prefers taking the easiest route, and the path it's most familiar with is the one it's travelled the most.

It's an incredibly controversial statement to make in today's society, but certain elements of your personality are more beliefs and habits than they are a reality. Whilst you may have anxiety from time to time, have ADHD, or work better at night than early morning, the *extent* to which you are these things is more the product of habit and grooves in your brain (which you've dug yourself) than your genetics. Depression, ADHD, OCD, and anxiety are all real states (there's no denying that), but the extent to which these mental dispositions are anchored to your selfhood is not as severe as you have led yourself to believe. You are more than your mental health, and you have so many options to take control of your life and mind through professional and personal help. You are not alone in how you feel, and you don't have to deal with what you're going through alone. Very few people in this world can live a depression-free, anxiety-free, procrastination-free, or stress-free life, and even fewer can live without any mental disturbance or difficulties. Everyone has pathways in their brain which are less beneficial than others, but just because a certain thought, feeling, or behaviour comes instinctively to them doesn't mean it's inherent and fixed. In fact, the undoing of these pathways is what cognitive-behavioural therapy is all about.

Your brain likes to trick you into believing you can't do certain things in life, particularly if you've suffered with a particular condition for an extensive period of time. However, the moment you listen to your brain and claim you can't do something because you're 'X' or you 'have Y', you sell yourself short and diminish your possibilities in the world by investing more in the habitual lies your brain tells you than the reality of your neuroplasticity. Unlike in childhood, when you inherently lacked the autonomy and capacity to make well-informed decisions or challenge your beliefs, you now have the ability to empower yourself by harnessing your brain's plasticity and overturning or mitigating the effects of your past by constructing positive neuroplasticity.

STOP COMPARING YOURSELF TO OTHERS

The third-most common reason why many people procrastinate is their tendency to compare themselves to others. There's no better way to make yourself feel inadequate in life than comparing yourself to other people, particularly to those who are in your field or who are living out the life you want. Comparison rarely inspires or motivates you as you would hope it would. The primary product of comparison is usually demoralisation. In today's society, the comparison trap is even more corrupt, thanks to social media. The only comparisons you can make are against picture-perfect highlight reels of other people's lives, Photoshopped and Facetuned bodies, and algorithmically pleasing success stories. Your comparison data is brutally distorted beyond the realms of reality, and even though you know all this, you still digest these images and become consumed with shame and self-hatred. Self-comparison occurs most acutely in domains most valuable to you, such as health, appearance, relationships, professions, wealth, and personal goals and interests. You can use Instagram to follow fitness influencers in the hopes they will inspire you to improve your health and fitness, or scroll through Pinterest to collect images of minimalist apartments to inspire your own home decor. However, self-corrosion occurs when you stop taking inspiration from what you see and instead only see the insurmountable differences between you and the other.

My wife, Karen, is a brilliant singer and musician; her life has always revolved around music, but she spent the majority of her working life in jobs which bored her to tears. The more she became sucked into the world of mundane work and stress, the less musically inspired she became and, over the years, she slowly retreated from the music world entirely. One night, I finally asked her why she had stopped pursuing her music ambitions, and her response was an assertive 'I'm not good enough' declaration.

Most people have told themselves they're not good enough because they've encountered tens of people in life who have made them feel that way. They've had relationships, friends, colleagues, teachers, and even family members who have knocked them down, judged them, and treated them like they're a piece of wet toilet paper stuck on their heel. Even though they know these people are unkind, they believe them. Judging from the way others have treated them, they start to believe they're not enough for the world, and the same thought process happens when they compare themselves to others.

When you see others who share the same interests, values, and professional pursuits as you become more successful in life, you subconsciously translate this information into the 'I'm not good enough' belief. This was what happened to my wife, Karen. I asked her who she 'wasn't good enough' in comparison to, and she immediately replied, 'Katy Perry and Taylor Swift'. The more I probed her, the more I came to realise that my wife was convinced that she'd never be as good at Taylor Swift or Katy Perry, even if she dedicated the next forty years of her life to singing.

Swift and Perry are two anomalies in the world; their lives are not reflective of that of a brilliant singer's, but because their names and faces are plastered everywhere, people believe they're much more relatable than they really are. Those two singers are just two names in a world of 7.53 billion names. Yes, they have talent, fame, fortune, and reputations, but they aren't reflective of all singers. Both Swift and Perry, like all famous and talented people in the world, got a lucky break. They were born at the right place, at the right time, to the right people; their talents and circumstances led them into spheres of influence which ultimately changed their lives forever. They are, undoubtedly, talented singers, but their status doesn't mean they are the best singers in the world. They're just two of the most famous ones. There are hundreds of thousands, if not millions, of singers in this world who would be considered better singers than Swift and Perry but never got discovered by a record label or never earned millions from their singing, but this doesn't mean they're not good enough. There are billions of authors out there whose works never get published, scientists who never win the Nobel prize, and incredible actors who will never set foot on a movie set. They are all more than good enough to be recognised, lauded, and famous, but just because they haven't attained great wealth or fame doesn't mean they're not good enough. The only reason my wife didn't think she would ever be as good as Katy Perry is because she knew she could never be Katy Perry. She would never have the same genetic makeup, philosophies, style, interest, personality, relationships, experiences, and voice. My wife is her own unique, talented self, but because she wasn't earning millions (or any money) as a musician, she didn't think she was good enough, and she stopped herself from even trying.

The comparison trap is infinite if you allow yourself to fall prey to it. There's an infinite number of people and dimensions to compare yourself to, meaning you'll always come out at the bottom. Being able to look at others through a lens of appreciation and equality rather than inferiority, jealousy, and defeatism requires you to start viewing people for who they are rather than what they have or what they've done. Once you start appreciating others for just being in the world, you can start appreciating and loving yourself for just being here as well.

As this chapter has established, there are tens of reasons as to why you procrastinate, and you will have unique vulnerabilities which cause you to do so, from low self-esteem to unhelpful beliefs about your abilities, boredom, and curiosity. Whatever the logic underlying your procrastination is, you have the ability to overcome it by implementing an appropriate strategy, such as establishing reinforcing routines into your day, practising gratitude and appreciation, setting yourself a deadline, changing your environment, or celebrating small wins. The key to overcoming your procrastination lies in your willingness to take the time to understand yourself more, practise self-compassion, and implement tailored strategies to remould the neuroplasticity of your unique mental wiring.

CHAPTER TWENTY-TWO

WORKING WITH A BLANK CANVAS

THE LAST CHAPTER IS WHERE PEOPLE HOPE TO FIND the answer. Most self-help books string people along to the last chapter, which finally reveals the ultimate ten steps that the reader needs to take to achieve X or the twelve rules to live a more effective life. Instead, I am going to use the last chapter to tell you the truth. No guru, life coach, or course is going to give you the magical formula to live the best life possible because there is no such thing. There aren't twelve steps you can take, and there aren't certain rules and rituals to follow which will give you the results you want. Life isn't that clear-cut.

You and your circumstances, goals, beliefs, values, and strengths are too unique to fit any formulaic plan laid out by some expert who has never met you. What someone accomplished in twelve steps may take someone else fifteen thousand steps, and the rituals which work best for one person won't suit every lifestyle or inherent difference. There's no way of getting it 'right' in life, and there's no 'right' way of living, so it's pointless to hope that someone has laid out the step-by-step guide to the ultimate way of living for you somewhere in the deep crevices of a book. I cannot tell you anything about who you are. I can't tell you when to get up in the morning, what diet you should be eating, what values you should be driven by, how you should go about actualising your ambitions, or what you should do to better your life today. All I can tell you is that optimal living hinges on a single principle: you get out of life what you work on, that is, you get what you practise.

Things aren't just going to show up for you in life: happiness won't come along in the shape of a partner, child, career, paycheque, or even as a feeling you are just hit with one day. Society tells you through films and advertising that happiness and fulfilment are the results of ideal circumstances where you have the job you love, you're in the best relationship you could ever want, everyone treats you nicely, and you're not in need or want of anything. This is why so many people sit around waiting for life to sort itself out: waiting for someone they hate to leave their company, waiting for their partner to change, waiting for a dream career opportunity, or waiting for their depression and anxiety to just go away. They believe circumstances and situations are a matter of time and believe happiness and fulfilment are products of natural intervention, which the universe and fate bestow upon them when they least expect it.

Society's marketing and Hollywood's depictions of happiness and fulfilment tell you the story that life is just waiting to happen to you because that's the idea they need to sell you. They need you to buy into the idea that life can change in an instant thanks to superficial circumstances and products because they can't make money off your internal experiences.

They can't profit off you practising gratitude, love, kindness, and authenticity. They can't profit from you taking action to deepen your relationships or living according to your values. Society would rather have you wait for them to come up with the solution for you than allow you to realise your happiness and fulfilment are the results of the choices you make in life.

Your optimal way of living can only be uncovered through you taking responsibility for your emotions and the thoughts which determine your behaviour. Your optimal performance will be the result of your understanding and living by your values, managing your emotions and thoughts, and ensuring you maintain and create meaningful relationships.

All you have in life are options, and the main options revolve around whether or not you put the principles you learn into practice and how and why you choose to do so. The options you have in life aren't limited by a number of steps or rules. Your options are infinite, but in order to not waste them, you need to stop impeding yourself by letting your mind and emotions tell you what you're not capable of. What I hope has become clear to you now is that success depends upon a strong foundation, and that foundation is you. Your emotional, physical, and mental well-being determine the quality of the outcomes you have in life, emphasis being on the word *quality*. Healthy mental, physical, and emotional well-being cannot prevent sudden, unexplained illnesses, tragedies, losses, financial difficulties, relationship issues, or career problems, but your well-being plays a crucial role in how these circumstances affect and impact your quality of life. Many experiences and circumstances you encounter in life will be entirely out of your control, but the *quality* of these outcomes is dependent on you and your degree of personal mastery. You have the autonomy and power to choose which pathways in your brain you want to starve or feed. You can either create self-imposed struggles by feeding the losses, oppression, poverty, illness, mental health issues, injustice, and discomfort, or you can starve them and feed the good you create and focus on in life.

DON'T SKIP AHEAD OF THE PROCESS

Many people finish reading a self-help book or listening to a podcast by some guru and feel inspired—not to change their lives, but to become influencers just like them. They want to be seen as important and famous enough to have bestselling books and popular podcasts, and be invited to give a TED Talk which will amass millions of views on YouTube. This is because people always fall back into the habit of adopting personal significance as their core value (as discussed in chapter six). People want to escape that painful feeling of emptiness and insignificance which haunts them, and they always believe the answer is outside of them in the form of some activity, career, relationship, or body shape. You're not going to find the life-changing magic to becoming a more successful and fulfilled person in any book, podcast, or TED Talk because nobody in this world can tell you what your core values are. Your core values are the unique essences which drive you forward in life to be your best self, but because they're not marketable products, gurus sell you pre-packaged, quick, and easy lifestyle hacks like rules, tactics, routines, and rituals, which will help you temporarily fill the void and help them earn some money. Taking cold showers in the morning won't make you a better parent, getting up at 5 am won't make you a millionaire, eating the carnivore diet won't make you a fitter person, and wearing a uniform every day won't strengthen your relationships. Whilst some little lifestyle quirks advised by gurus can make you feel better, stronger, more awake, focused, or in the zone, they're not going to make you into the person you aspire to be.

Aspiring to become an influencer before developing steadfast personal mastery is like aspiring to run a marathon on broken legs. Just as you're instructed by flight attendants to put on your own oxygen mask first before you assist others to put on theirs, you can only help others once you are in the best shape possible, mentally, spiritually, and physically. It is not selfish or egotistical to prioritise working on yourself first before you extend yourself to help others grow and develop. On the contrary, it would be nothing but amoral and disingenuous to do otherwise. You will never be effective at influencing others until you are effective at influencing yourself.

Rebelling against the norm and taking responsibility for yourself in life isn't about proving yourself to others. It's about getting out of your own way so you may construct what you want without self-imposed limitations. You're responsible for freeing yourself from your self-imposed captivity and struggle. Blaming others for who, how, and where you are today is not only disempowering but dishonest. Nobody forces you to think, feel, or be the way you are today. People played roles in influencing the choices you made about how you felt, thought, and behaved, but no one forced you to think, be, or feel the way you do. When you were a child, you were more susceptible to influence, but as an adult, you have no excuses. Your memories, circumstances, and learned beliefs should not hold the monopoly over your life as they currently do, and if you want more from your life and yourself, you need to take the reins and practise the principles laid out in this book and beyond. There is a huge distinction between what shows up in life (circumstances, illnesses, events, people, etc.) and what you practise in response; you can either practise blame, pity, sadness, depression, negative thinking, and defeatism, or you can practise authenticity, purposefulness, honesty, openness, responsibility, and emotional stability and take control of your life rather than allow circumstances to control you and what you're capable of being.

DO YOUR BEST, DON'T TRY YOUR BEST

Everyone on this planet wants to change, but very few people are willing to. Most people resist change through excuses such as 'I don't know how to change' or 'I tried to change but it didn't work'. Claiming that you don't know how to change or what you're willing to change is just an excuse to conceal from yourself and those around you your resistance to change, and to 'try' something is not the same as being willing to do something. 'Trying' is nothing more than the desire for credit for something you didn't intend to do (as highlighted poignantly by master Yoda: 'Do...or do not. There is no try').

Only you know who you are willing to become today for the rest of your life. You know who you want to become for your friends, partner, children, siblings, family, colleagues, and society, and you know what you're willing to do to become that person. You know whether or not you're willing to let go of being right, shift from entitlement to appreciation, stop gossiping, change your perspective and see the other side, change your beliefs, take your commitments seriously, let go of the past and its hurts, forgive those who wronged you, share your authentic feelings, listen and learn more than defend your ego, stop blaming others, take responsibility, and stop criticising yourself.

Becoming the person you aspire to be is very different from

dreaming of being that way. To grow into someone who is inspirational, effective, influential, helpful, loving, accepting, and skilled requires dedication, passion, and intent: these qualities don't come about by accident or with age. In order to become great, you need to ask yourself important questions and refine your mind. What do you accept, and what do you dismiss? What do you have time for, and what don't you have time for? What things do you give up on, and what do you pursue fervently? What kinds of things do you take seriously, and what do you consider a waste of time? What inspires you and sparks creativity, and what drains you? Knowing who you are willing to become for yourself and other people helps you identify what you are and are not willing to change about yourself. You know deep down who you need to become in order to get the results you want in life. You know what actions that version of you needs to take, what thoughts you invest in, and how you manage your relationships and emotions.

OVERCOME YOUR PRIDE AND BE HUMBLE

Being willing to change requires getting over your pride. As Carl Jung said, 'Through pride we are ever deceiving ourselves. But deep down below the surface of the average conscience a still, small voice says to us, something is out of tune.' Your ego likes to defend you against this little voice in order to protect you from guilt and shame, but this pride gets in the way of you becoming your best self.

Even the most under-confident and self-loathing of people suffer from pride; nobody likes admitting they were wrong or that they've been living incongruently and inefficiently for potentially years of their life. People cling to their bad habits, negative mindsets, emotions, and behaviours out of an unconscious pride. After years of being the way they are and feeling the way they have, they don't want to admit to themselves that they don't have to be, feel, or think this way. It's embarrassing to tell yourself you can choose not to be anxious, depressed, angry, helpless, sad, destructive, lonely, or defeated, which is why people get defensive about the idea and reject it as stupidity, nonsense, and unrelatable. They proudly cling to their labels, claiming no one can possibly understand their hardship and what they've experienced in life. If that's how you feel, be that way. Enjoy living the life that's not fulfilling you; enjoy waiting around for your brain to suddenly click into gear and make it all better again; enjoy wallowing in your labels and excuses. No one in this world is going to force you to be anything or anyone you're not willing to be. You can cling to your emotions and way of being as long as you want and live life as you have done for the rest of your days. Or, if you want more for yourself in life, you can take action by starting with just a small sentence: 'Even though I feel _____, I am willing to feel _____ instead; I am willing to change and grow; I am willing to experience life differently.' This one little sentence can be used for every aspect of your life, from what you're willing to feel, to what you're willing to do, think, and be.

BE YOUR AUTHENTIC SELF

After finishing this book, you may feel inspired and ignited to go out there and start your business, work on your relationships, change your career, or build a community, but there's no point going out and doing anything in life unless you are willing to start expressing yourself authentically and begin representing who you truly are, and this takes time to develop. Most people have decades of unlearning to manage and self-exploration to undergo because they have no idea who they truly are underneath the layers upon layers of social constructs they've adopted subconsciously. Before you go out and start building, you need to unearth who you truly are outside of your gender, career, sexual orientation, role, labels, hobbies, and dreams. Your labels, looks, money, and the dreams you never dared to bring to fruition have absolutely no meaning in this world outside your own ego. The labels you assign to yourself don't change the world; being proud of your body doesn't change the world; being good at your job doesn't change the world, and won't change the world after you're long gone. You are only ever going to be determined in life by the legacy you leave behind and the lives you invest in. If you want to be remembered as someone who truly stood for something that was bigger than themselves, bigger than their labels, job, and interests, you need to decide to commit to something which goes beyond the scope of your feelings, wants, and needs.

POUR YOURSELF INTO LIFE ONE STEP AT A TIME

If you truly want to positively influence people and leave a memorable legacy behind, you need to build a tribe who learn from you how to better understand themselves and see what they're capable of being and doing in the world. However, there's no use in forming a tribe of people to influence and inspire if you haven't produced the results for yourself. People are very rarely interested in words; they're interested in action and results. You can read all the books about self-development, success, personal growth, and empowerment, but unless you have the results for yourself, no one is going to be interested in your theories and well-structured opinions.

You need to choose one aspect of your life, and only one aspect (for now), to drive and hyperfocus your value system upon.

You need to be willing and brave enough to fully commit to living congruently and authentically in this aspect of your life, regardless of whether it's your career, relationships, or mental health, and just pour every ounce of who you are into it. Once you know what it feels like to live to this degree of purposefulness in one area of your life, you can start expanding your horizons and unleashing your more empowered self upon all aspects of life. You cannot honestly help others before you master all elements of your life and approach each one with the same degree of emotional stability, confidence, self-worth, and authenticity.

WHAT ARE YOU GOING TO DO ABOUT IT?

Over the past couple of years, you may have read another twelve books on psychology and personal development written by some of the world's experts in their field, you may have taken a dozen online courses, and you may have listened to hours upon hours of podcasts run by some of the world's leading figures in personal development and economics. You've read a lot and studied what the experts have said and done over the past few years, and to this, I ask: so what?

So what? What does it mean to the rest of the world that you've read all these books and taken those courses? What does it mean to your family, relationships, career, ambitions, and society that you know a little more about personal development and success? As I stated earlier, knowledge isn't powerful unless it's implemented. Knowledge is of no use to you or anyone around you if you consume it and sit on it; knowledge needs to be applied and shared in order to bring about change in the world.

There are so many things in life which people aren't happy

with: their jobs, their relationships, political systems, the environment, their bodies, human rights, taxes, council spending, animal welfare, premature deaths, violence, crime, mental health services, and the price of healthcare in general. They'll read articles about all these things online, share them on their Facebook walls, and re-tweet them with additional angry commentary; they'll go home and rant about them to their friends and partners and potentially even lose sleep over them. They'll worry about the state of the world around them, cry over it, yell about it, engage in heated debates about it with their family over dinner...and that's it. They'll rant and rave and cry but expect someone else, somewhere else, to pick up the pieces for them and sort it all out.

People are more willing to complain than do anything about their circumstances. They tell themselves they're just one person so they can't possibly do anything about it, meanwhile waiting for one person somewhere out there to do it for them. You are just as capable of inciting change and creating meaningful and significant change as you expect others to be. Stop waiting around for someone else to fix you and fix all the issues you have in the world. If you don't agree with something and you want to see something change, what are you willing to do about it? What are you willing to do with all the information you gathered, the opinions you agree or disagree with, the politics which make you angry, or the parts of your life you know are making you unhappy? Are you willing to just complain about them for another two, five, or ten years, or are you willing to take action, make changes, and start producing results?

The only way you can start designing a blueprint for your life is by making a decision about which steps you're willing to take to conquer the mountains you want to climb. You can't waste any more of your life waiting for life to mould around your delicate circumstances and needs. You need to start making decisions about who you want to rise up and become in the world as it is. If you want to improve the calibre of your relationship, you need to stop waiting for the other person to change and instead ask yourself who you need to start being today to see a difference. Do you need to start being more loyal, more transparent, and more sincere, or do you need to be more academic, richer, thinner, more toned, or better looking?

If you are currently unhappy with the state of your life at the moment, chances are you are channelling energy into meaningless fields and pursuits which aren't producing the changes you truly want in life. The choices you make determine the outcomes you desire, meaning there is no use going to the gym to save your relationship when what you're starving for is better communication, and it is futile to waste hours of your life trying to get likes on social media when all you want is a more meaningful and higher-paying career. Unless your goals and pursuits in life are values-driven, you will find yourself sucked into a vortex of unfulfilment, temporary happiness, and boredom. You need to take a moment and start analysing whether or not your priorities lie within or outside your comfort zone. Those of you who see risk as an enemy to be avoided are going to live very passive and unproductive lives. Your best life and best self lies beyond the comfort zone, and all you can do in life is keep extending yourself out further and further to reap the rewards of living life to your fullest potential.

When you rebel against what you've been programmed to believe and start taking responsibility for your life, you begin to conquer all of your endeavours. If your endeavours are anything less than values-based, they are incongruent, and they will ultimately lead to nothing. Even if you achieve the goals you have in life which aren't values-based, you will still feel starved of true inner peace and fulfilment. To rebel against the life you're living is to own who you are, be who you are, and commit the rest of your life to striving to always be who you are willing to become.

ACKNOWLEDGMENTS

Mum and Dad, thank you for getting me started in life.

Pete and Carol Hope, thank you, I will eternally be appreciative for you steering me in this direction.

A.R Bernard, thank you, you unknowingly gave structure to my thinking.

Gerard Egan, thank you for helping me to understand life complexities, simplistically.

Karen, you're my best friend, and with you, the process is so thoroughly worthwhile.

Julian, Debby, Bernard, Toni-Lee, Tina, Tarique, Lesley, Ed and Larry, thank you all for reminding me that the team 'works'.

Naysayers, thank you for unceasingly pouring fuel on the fire.

ABOUT THE AUTHOR

KAIN RAMSAY is the top-ranked psychology and personal growth instructor at Udemy and founder of Achology. com, an academy devoted to teaching modern methods and principles of applied psychology. Known for his trademark teaching style, Kain delivers highly sought-after programs that include Mindfulness, Life Coaching, Cognitive Behavior Therapy, and Neuro-Linguistic Programming. In 2018, he partnered with world-renowned author Gerard Egan to produce an online adaptation of Egan's international bestselling book, *The Skilled Helper*.

Kain launched his career in the military and has more than fifteen years of experience in marketing, business development, and modern applied psychology. He lives in Dunfermline, Scotland with his wife, Karen.